Red Hot Radio

Sex, Violence and Politics
at the
End of the American Century

Saul Landau

Common Courage Press   Monroe, Maine

E
885
.L366
1998

Library of Congress Cataloging-in-Publication Data
Landau, Saul
Red hot radio: sex, violence and politics
at the end of the American century/Saul Landau;
foreword by Barbara Ehrenreich.
p. cm.
Includes index.
ISBN 1-56751-147-3 (cloth). -- ISBN 1-56751-146-5 (pbk.).
1. United States--Politics and government--1993- 2. United
States--Social conditions--1980- I. Title.
E885.L366 1998
973.929--dc21
CIP

Common Courage Press
Box 702
Monroe, ME 04951

www.commoncouragepress.com

207-525-0900   fax: 207-525-3068

First Printing

Acknowledgments

This diary-like approach to the world would not have been possible without the help of many people. I thank Elisabeth Blankenhorn and Sonia Angulo, who worked tirelessly to help prepare the manuscript and offered insightful editing suggestions. Engineers Mike Corgan and Rick Cass used their expertise to facilitate numerous broadcasts. My colleagues at Cal Poly, especially the staff at ITAC, gave me great support. Deans Lev Gonick and Barbara Way made possible the space, time and atmosphere to do many of the commentaries. Similarly, the staff and fellows of the Institute for Policy Studies in Washington, D.C., especially Marcus Raskin, pushed me to clarify, and to keep doing my commentaries. Scott Armstrong and Phil Brenner listened and gave me tough and sound recommendations on numerous occasions.

Thanks to my intern, Reanne, who made a great effort to discipline me. My Pacifica Radio colleagues, especially Julie Drizin, Patricia Guadalupe, Mark Bevis and Laura Flanders provided direction and motivation. Haskell Wexler and Carol Ferry provided me with ongoing encouragement.

Rebecca Switzer has proven to be the most honest, best and toughest editor of my life. I would be at a loss without her. Naturally, I alone am responsible for mistakes and judgements and any other problems readers find in this book. So, sock it to me!

Foreword

By Barbara Ehrenreich

Often I am stopped on the street by earnest people who inquire, "Left, right—shouldn't we be over all those isms by now? Here we have a fine youngish president of no known political convictions building us a bridge—a toll bridge, true enough, but nevertheless—to the 21st century, and you keep going on about these obsolete categories left over from the long-dead 18th! In this era of Web marketing, telecommunications and universal acclaim for the global free enterprise system, how can we be expected to tell the difference between left and right anyway?"

In response to these queries I say two things. One: How do you manage to get your shoes on the correct feet in the morning or, for that matter, decide which hand should wield the fork? And two: Read Saul Landau.

I've known Saul for over 15 years, as a colleague, mentor and friend. He's not a political scientist or theoretician. He won't bore you with Marxist macro-economics or befuddle you with fancy post-modernist dissections of "difference." He's just a living, breathing exemplar of what it means to be left, as opposed to right, or (no bias here) morally and intellectually alive, as opposed to brain-dead and socially clueless.

And what it means, as you will soon discover in the pages that follow, is, first of all, using your God-given noodle. I suspect that Landau is smarter than most of us, but he's also smart enough to show us how the thinking process works, and it generally starts with a blink and a resounding "Huh?" A War on Drugs led by martini-swigging bureaucrats? Welfare "reform" to get the poor out of their homes and onto the streets? An arms build-up without an enemy in sight? As the rap group Public Enemy once succinctly put it, "Don't believe the hype." The first duty of a radical is to exposé naked emperors and half-dressed lies, and Landau does this in inimitable street-corner style.

But being a radical is not the same as being a wise-ass—although, in this era of fradulent pieties and sanctimonious cruelty, being a wise-ass certainly helps. The other defining dimension of the left is moral one, and it operates more like a reflex than a rule: In every fight, you side with the underdog, even when the overdogs are much bigger and more numerous than you. For a journalist, this means, first of all, that you don't choose as your topics the exercise regimens of the stars or the investment habits of CEOs. You look at life from the other side, where the downtrodden, deprived and discriminated against dwell. You write, as Landau does, about who's trampling on them, and what the tramplees are doing to fight back, whether they're Mayan villagers in southern Mexico, immigrants beaten by border cops, or blue-collar folks in the de-industrialized Midwest. Because you understand that in one way or another—because you're gay or female, black or some other shade of "non-white," very young or very old—you're an underdog too, and the underdogs are your pack.

It follows that all conventional political categories can be elucidated with reference to a straightofrward and vivid case-in-point: You are walking down the street and come across a group of bullies kicking a man (or a woman or a child) who is lying on the ground. If you are a liberal, you will feel concern and walk off musing about the possibility of legislation to prevent such nasty doings. If you are a conservative, you will nod apporvingly and surmise that the fellow on the ground must have done something pretty nasty himself to deserve such vigorous corporal punish-ment. But if you are a radical or a leftist—even a frail one and out of shape, you have no choice but to wade in and take on the bul-lies yourself. (If you are a reactionary of course, you will dash off and buy yourself some steel-tipped boots so you can join in the fun.)

This analogy helps explain why it is possible for so many people to grow up in America, achieve literacy and numeracy, hold a job, perhaps even get their shoes on right in the morning—without having the slightest notion of what it might mean to be radical or left. In a word, the means of communication are, for the most part, owned and controlled by the bullies, their pals and immediate subalterns. Hence a spectrum of media punditry that generally ranges from moderate conservative to proto-facist reactionary. Hence also the iron-clad media rule all writers and TV producers are required to memorize: Make it upbeat and make it upscale! Forget the guy being beaten in the gutter and focus on the heartaches and difficult cosmetic surgery decisions faced by the bullying class.

Fortunately, there's one more thing that defines a radical: She or he doesn't give up. When they take away her pen, she writes in crayon, or blood. When they ban her from the radio, she scoots over to the Internet. When they take away her PC, she resorts to graffiti. Landau, more than anyone I can think of, does it all—poetry, journalism, radio, film, print—with erudition and mensch-like good humor. Read him, underdogs of the world, and delight!

Saul Landau

History Is Bunk

August 14, 1995

"History is bunk," declared Henry Ford. Most people don't understand that they are the accumulation of what has gone before them. Americans tend to deny the importance of history, while fighting ferociously to control the historical record—whether over why Harry Truman ordered the nuclear bombing of Japan or why women, blacks and other minorities merit affirmative action programs.

History offers parallels, periods to learn from—if we dare. By the late 1870s, Reconstruction had begun to give way to reaction. And white reactionaries questioned the newly-won rights of black Americans—as they do now.

By the 1890s, racist social commentators extolled the virtues of genteel, southern slave-holding civilization and condemned the liberating laws adopted during the post civil war period. The Supreme Court turned the Fourteenth Amendment into a document that afforded undeserved legal protection to the modern business corporation rather than a charter to insure former slaves a measure of real equality.

In the early 1890s, the corporate elite waged assaults against black rights and working class organizations—divide and rule. In the depression of the 1890s, the bosses feared that militant workers would seize their factories as they had done in France two decades earlier during the Paris Commune. Thus, the fearful burghers constructed strategically located regiment armories so that the National Guard could block the path of the rebelling workers and fire at them.

Political campaigners at the turn of the century invented Jim Crow language, which some tacked onto populist rhetoric—just as the mountebanks do now.

The Pete Wilsons (California governor) of a hundred years ago, also working for corporate interests, evoked fearful images of foreigners and racial minorities for the purpose of dividing working people. Corporations then and now seek the same end: reduce the socially necessary cost of labor.

Contemporary charlatans claim we have solved racial discrimination—as they promote racism under the name of anti-discrimination. Have they no shame, those "silver tongued orators," as William Jennings Bryan called them, those people who imply that the unfortunate get what's coming to them?

In the 1890s, Republicans gloated when company goons and police broke labor strikes. In 1995, Newt's troglodytes declared a great day for America when the House passed a bill cutting spending for the needy. California Democrat George Miller took the podium. "It's a great day," he said to the Newties, "if you're a fascist."

Miller referred to the hundred years of struggle it took for blacks and progressive whites to regain the moral and legal high ground they lost after Reconstruction. Courageous women and labor leaders struggled to reverse the corporate-segregationist course that began in the post-reconstruction period. And as labor and minorities won victories, all Americans began to amplify their understanding of rights.

In a year and a half, the Republican-dominated Congress has reversed some of those hard fought gains in fact, but not yet in consciousness. Political focus often depends on how secure we feel with our past, with history. In the coming years, before the history books about our lifetimes are rewritten in our lifetimes, we have a chance to define the context of our times, if we embrace history and act to protect the very rights that our ancestors won in struggle. In other words, if we prove that history is not bunk.

Saul Landau

Attention, Fish Lovers!

September 4, 1995

Fishing: a wholesome endeavor, pursued by healthy people. Ernest Hemingway's Nick put his hand in the cold lake water—and it was good. Nick's father casts, the fish bites. The two males, camping at the edge of the pine forest, cook and eat the pike. A unique male-bonding satisfaction that Hemingway's sexually-retarded men experienced when they convened with Nature around the theme of fishing. Yes, the river ran through it, all right.

And don't forget that time-honored macho view of innate goodness: standing hip deep in a freezing stream waiting for a fish to slash its mouth on the hook. Well, even some women now share this aesthetic—and kids of both sexes.

My early association with fish dates to when my mother forced a daily dose of cod liver oil down my throat. Years later I thanked her for torturing me with those spoonfuls of viscous slime extracted from the liver of a healthy cod.

So, imagine how a life-long fishing maven like myself felt when I read that Carol Browner, the EPA administrator, declared 40% of America's rivers, lakes and streams unsuitable for fishing. "Health advisories" about fish in U.S. inland waters have risen 20% in the last two years. A recently released federal study, according to the *New York Times*, warns the public to limit the consumption of fish caught in local waters.

New York health authorities say you can eat half a pound of fish from New York rivers and lakes weekly and still not die of poisoning. Don't panic! Republicans in Congress dismiss this sissy liberal report. They rewrote the Clean Water Act. If the act passes the Senate, big, bad government won't have power to enforce laws on sewage treatment or industrial discharges. Republicans sympathize with the victims of government regulation—you guessed it—the large, polluting industries that contribute to their campaigns. Thus motivated, Newt's legions prepare to scrap wimpy regulations like the Great Lakes

7

Initiative—which was intended to keep a few fish swimming in those five basins. After three decades of efforts to decontaminate them, the Great Lakes remain ecologically inharmonious for people, fish and plants.

The Newtie Cuties would bar the EPA from fining the states for not enforcing environmental rules on inland waters. The *New York Times* calls this "an invitation to the states to start backsliding."

So fellow fishermen and women, forget ideologies. Stand firm before the common enemy. Mercury particles from chemical wastes find their way into the fish we catch and eat. No wonder we feel lousy.

We fish worshipers must rely on the Senate to block the House-sponsored deregulation. Are we less than confident about our fishing futures? Picture a central-casting angler in a sludge-filled mountain stream holding a mutant creature! Hemingway, are you turning over in your grave?

Saul Landau

Kunstler Obit

September 5, 1995

I felt vulnerable when I heard that William Kunstler, age 76, had died in New York when his heart gave out. Now there's one less person to defend me in case I'm arrested. His antagonists accused him of being a publicity hound. Kunstler admitted enjoying the spotlight, but his purpose, he said, "is to keep the state from becoming all-domineering, powerful."

Kunstler used the limelight to make points on justice and the evil of the state on TV with sound bites as he would emerge from courtrooms or in lectures to large audiences. In court, his barbs often showed that the judge had no robes.

Like early American revolutionaries who rebelled against the British Crown, Kunstler saw government as base. "My role," he declared, "is always be a burr under the saddle. That's all. There is no real revolution."

No, Kunstler was not a revolutionary—although he flirted with it in the 1960s when he represented revolutionaries like Dr. Martin Luther King Jr. and the Chicago Seven. I'll never forget Kunstler's repartee with semi-senile judge Julius Hoffman, who made no secret of his aversion for the accused. A laugh is not a crime, he instructed the judge, when the defendants and the audience in the courtroom burst out laughing at Hoffman's fatuousness.

Kunstler viewed criminal cases as political because he believed that the state induced crime. This anarchist bent prompted him to defend clients who most progressives considered criminals.

Besides defending Stokely Carmichael, Lenny Bruce and Daniel Berrigan, Kunstler also defended Mafiosos like John Gotti and Jack Ruby; inmates who rebelled at Attica Prison in New York; and Colin Ferguson, who shot up a Long Island commuter train.

Kunstler was not the perpetually angry person that the media often presented him as. When attacked, however, his tiger came out, but that only when he had a good lawyer's reason. Kunstler turned his anger on and off when it served his client's purpose, or when he thought emotion would instruct a judge on law or, more important, on justice.

Kunstler had little interest in making big fees or in conforming to the sartorial dictates of bourgeois society. A lawyer who shared a hotel room with him offered to send Kunstler's shirts to the laundry, but Kunstler insisted that when he was out of town on a case he always wore the same shirt for three days.

This would-be poet and joke teller assumed his role as defender of pariahs when he was in his middle forties. "I was bored," he said of his more routine law practice.

Progressives should understand that Bill Kunstler tried to keep open the political and intellectual spaces that the government is perpetually trying to shut down.

Boy, will we miss him!

Saul Landau

Conversion Is Not Heresy

September 9, 1995

Last week the House majority forced the Pentagon to buy more B2 bombers than even the most hawkish generals wanted—while simultaneously making massive cuts in spending on the poor, sick and elderly.

I'm not going to bum out you listeners. Yes, the defense lobby celebrated yet another triumph for unnecessary war spending. But Vermont's Bernie Sanders, the House's sole Independent, also won his amendment to the Defense Appropriations Bill that cut off the Pentagon's ability to pay bonuses to defense CEOs.

Are you shocked to discover that the Department of Defense paid your taxpayer's dollars as rewards to weapons contractors—just for merging?!

In March, Martin Marietta and Lockheed top execs agreed that they merited $92 million in bonuses. After all, the largest defense contractors merging is a history-making event. The Pentagon showed its approval of this unprecedented corporate coitus by contributing $31 million of our money. A 1994 law had opened the door for the Pentagon to encourage defense companies to downsize and re-structure, i.e., fire workers and merge. The corporate slickies of Lockheed and Martin shut down a dozen factories and labs and laid off over 19,000 workers. The CEOs got handsome bonuses.

Thanks to the Sanders amendment, Congress cut off one egregious form of corporate welfare. But what about the laid-off workers? Ironically, both pacifists and corporate execs agree about the need for conversion. But the corporate idea of swords into ploughshares converts the employed into the unemployed. Peace activists naturally welcome the closing of weapons factories, but also believe that laid-off defense workers should receive other jobs.

Their idea of conversion is to make weapons factories into peaceful goods production plants! But there's not a lot of that going on. One exception is the Fort Ord army base, near

Monterey, California, which has been transformed into a new university. OK, so the army left poison on the land from buried ordinance and spilled fuel. And the Pentagon, which happily paid bonuses to the defense company executives, refuses to spend its easily earned money to clean up the mess it left. There's no justice!

So, here's my proposal. For every dollar Congress allocates for weapons and other trivia, it authorizes an equal amount for conversion— including clean up of old bases and defense plants. Such a plan would increase the budget by 50%, of course, so to compensate, Congress should reduce spending on the military by 50%. Thus, the overall defense allocation would be the same as it is now—about $245 billion. However, half of it would go to pay laid-off defense workers to do better things.

Or Congress could authorize the Pentagon to give bonuses to newly-fired people who once manufactured their weapons instead of to unworthy CEOs. You think I'm being a little utopian?

Saul Landau

Welfare Reform—the New Cruelty

September 19, 1995

In the 1930s President Franklin Roosevelt declared one third of our nation ill fed, ill clothed and ill housed. Government, he decided, must help those that capitalism had cast out.

In those dark, depression days, only the Ebenezer Scrooges blamed the victims. The economic system collapsed. The Great depression, as my daughter might say, was a bummer. Those who lived through it no longer trusted the private sector with public economic security. The depression demonstrated capitalism's cruel indifference. And millions of people logically became socialists. But not Roosevelt—he used the federal government to prop up capitalism, while simultaneously helping its victims.

Thirty years later, in the 1960s, President Lyndon Johnson continued Roosevelt's project to end poverty in America. Johnson mobilized anew the federal government, but his design also called for community action, community development, and participation of the poor. Well, not to worry, that part didn't happen. And the amount spent on the Great Society paled before military expenditures.

Welfare evolved over this sixty-year period into a bare survival system for the unemployed, for mothers with children but no support, for those fired and without access to unemployment insurance, and for those disabled but not yet on disability.

The Republican Party, backed by a number of Democrats and the president, now vows to eliminate welfare and destroy the instruments created to help the system's victims. "Welfare doesn't work," they announce. It hasn't moved millions of people into decent-paying jobs. It fosters dependency.

Republicans use "welfare recipient" as a euphemism for black and Hispanic poor. "Welfare cheat" refers to people who receive meager checks to support families. The revolutionary Republicans, the new-age Darwinians, want to return the welfare mandate to the states—knowing they have less money for the needy, and lack the ability to raise it.

Yes, welfare stinks, it creates dependency. Work is better. But capitalism downsizes, takes away jobs, lowers wages and benefits. Most members of Congress don't remember the depression. They cavalierly pass subsidies for oil drillers, tobacco growers, home buyers. Washington's "K" Street lobbyist welfare kings suck up millions in phony consultancies. Most welfare reformers are white and beneficiaries of accumulated wealth, not accumulated despair. Most receive campaign contributions from industries whose profits derive from cutting the socially necessary cost of labor. Where will welfare mothers work? Who will take care of the kids? Not our problem, says Congress. Those who have, deserve; the poor had their chance and blew it.

As lobbyists with open checkbooks dance through congressional halls, where are representatives of the multi millions who will be more ill fed, ill housed and ill clad if Congress passes its welfare reform? Will FDR's and LBJ's ghosts haunt members of Congress—and residents of the White House?

What kind of society takes dignity from the poor? Why can't the richest society in world care for its victims?

Saul Landau

Evicted Santa

December 20, 1995

I've been trying to understand neo-liberalism, free market economics, and the meaning of private property. Little did I suspect that my teacher would be a man who was just 86ed from a Westland, Michigan shopping mall. He has a long white beard—that looks false—wears a red suit and hat and appears to have a cushion stuffed next to his tummy. He says, "Ho Ho Ho," and rings a bell next to a collection pot. OK, you guessed his identity, but why evict a Salvation Army, shopping-mall Santa—just as the Christmas spirit arrives to make people soft touches for these universally accepted do-gooders?

"The answer," Santa told me, "is private property."

"Huh?" I respond. "A massive shopping mall with hundreds of thousands of citizens is private property? Next thing, the government will declare sidewalks and air private as well."

"Seriously," Santa continued, "in 1992, Supreme Court Justice Clarence Thomas wrote that property owners at malls can bar union organizers from using their property to distribute literature or talk to workers. To insure even-handedness, the Court included all outsiders."

"But Santa, collecting for the poor and for recovering alkies and drug addicts, is considered an outsider?" I protest.

"Listen," Saint Nick whispered, "Kmart, Sears and Toys R Us lawyers, for example, say that in order to keep out United Food and Commercial Workers Union representatives, you can't let in other groups—like Salvation Army Santas. That's fairness under the law. If you don't want sales clerks and stock people talking to unions about rotten working conditions, low pay and no benefits, then you can't let shoppers mix with Santa Claus."

"Wait a minute. This is ridiculous," I say. "A mall builder pours concrete over land so rain can't soak in to replenish ground water supply. He invites giant multi-national chains to occupy space in this auto-access, commercial center that destroys neighborhood shopping. Then the corporate headquarters of these

15

chains, who contribute mightily to Republican coffers, get a court decision that makes them like God, saying who can and cannot to do on this land."

"Hey," said Santa, "that's freedom." According to Clarence Thomas and the Republican majority in Congress, anything that interferes with your God-given rights to build an eyesore in a community and keep your sales staff from learning that by organizing they could earn more than $5.00 an hour and have time to go potty smacks of liberal corruption, if not downright communism, or hippie drug addiction or whatever they're calling it this year.

I sighed in despair. I won't shop at any mall that bars Salvation Army Santas—or union organizers. But what a dilemma! Where will I buy my daughter the new Christmas doll that eats with you at the table then says, "Excuse me," and throws up?

Saul Landau

Polonius and the Budget

January 5, 1996

As I tried to penentrate the debate between the Republican-led Congress and the Democratic president, I ran into an economist who consults for the government.

"What does a balanced budget mean?" I asked.

"Remember Polonius," he said. " 'Neither a borrower nor a lender be.' "

"What a dreamer!" I said. "U.S. consumers owe almost $400 billion—that's a third more than the entire defense budget. Suppose everyone paid off his bills, mortgages and home equity loans at the same time and vowed never again to owe a penny?"

"That would be subversive," he responded. "It would undermine the American economy and cause catastrophe."

"OK, then why shouldn't the federal government continue to owe money, like most governments throughout the world?"

"Look, this isn't about a balanced budget, but about a principle. The real issue is tax cuts. How much richer do the rich deserve to be? The Republican hard liners, revolutionaries, zealots, freshmen—call them anything but late for dinner—demand $240 billion in tax cuts that would benefit those who already have the lion's share of the nation's wealth."

"What's the principle in this?" I asked.

"The principle is: don't bite the hand that feeds you; he who pays the piper calls the tune and all that."

"Are you saying that these Republicans are nothing but paid tools of the rich?"

"Not all the rich. Only those who actually got in on last year's game. If you walked the halls of Congress or stepped inside congressional offices you would have noticed industry lobbyists in record numbers, some of them busy writing laws while seated at the congresspeople's desks. Indeed, one member of Congress invited an industry lobbyist to sit on the dais at a public hearing about regulating the very industry the lobbyist

17

represented. Even Bob Dole is a little ashamed of how some of his fellow Republicans are behaving."

"What do the Democrats want?" I asked.

"Clinton wants to win in '96 and, if a political miracle occurs, the Democrats might retake the House—especially if the media continues to beat up on these revolutionary Republicans."

"I'm confused," I said, "what makes them revolutionary?"

"Nothing," he said. "They're dyed-in-the-wool reactionaries, dedicated to screwing the poor out of every conceivable penny and handing it over to the rich. But they have coined Jeffersonian language—against a strong state and all that—and made the Democrats look like followers of Alexander Hamilton who want to maintain a strong central government."

"So, what do you predict?"

"Remember Polonius!" he declared as he ran off.

Wait, wasn't Polonius the fool hiding behind the curtain who took Hamlet's sword right in the belly? Who will be the Polonius of '96? Hmn. I fear it's me and my fellow citizens.

Saul Landau

ABCs of Tobacco Reporting

January 10, 1996

On Sunday, January 7, the *Washington Post* reporter Benjamin Weiser offered an anatomy of a network news mistake. ABC had discovered that the tobacco industry was adding more nicotine and vanillin to cigarettes, but its reporters proved a tad too eager.

ABC relied on "Deep Cough," a tobacco industry insider, who told them how the companies save money by adding reconstituted tobacco to real tobacco. The reconstituted stuff contains nicotine—but not new nicotine, the tobacco companies said. In fact, it had less nicotine than whole leaf tobacco.

So, when ABC's *Day One* said that Philip Morris "spiked" the cigarettes, the multi-national tobacco giant sued. At this point, the lawyers for both corporations entered the fray.

Was the spiking story true? If so, Philip Morris was adding even more addictive substances to better hook prospective smokers. The smoking company said that it wasn't necessary to add anything that wasn't originally there.

Lawyers spent tens of thousands of hours preparing documents and taking depositions—not to prove that smoking was or wasn't disease causing, but only to show that ABC's contention of spiking was false.

ABC surrendered and agreed to cover $15 million of Philip Morris' legal fees. Journalists felt a chill when the news giant settled with the tobacco giant and many blamed the cave-in on the ABC-Disney merger that occurred last summer. The big multinationals now have a hand in most businesses.

The amiable mouse that now directs ABC rehired Walt Bogdanich, the ABC producer, who stuck by his story. Pluto the puppy had no compunction about paying off the tobacco companies—well, their lawyers anyway. And Disney animals are all courteous, so they apologized to the poor, maligned tobacco company.

Philip Morris published the apology in full page ads. For them the settlement represented Divine Redemption. Spike their cigarettes with extra nicotine? Perish the thought! They even advise teenagers not to smoke, while their ads tell them how wonderful smoking is. Choice is the essence of democracy!

Philip Morris merely supplies the poor addicts with their weed. It's not like illegal drugs. They pay taxes, get subsidies and make immense contributions to political campaigns—that's the American way of life.

Sure, everyone knows tobacco kills. Yet ABC caved in on the advice of the nation's best lawyers, graduates from Ivy League law schools. Their choice clients, like cigarette companies and ABC, pay hundreds per hour billed—plus some nifty lunches.

It's our system—under law and all that. The ABC executives—who paid up—still believe in their reporters who "had a terrific story and pressed it one step too far." A news report slandered a mass murderer? Wait, what constitutes mass? Experts quibble over whether tobacco kills 400,000 a year or a hundred thousand more or less. Until we get exact figures, I wouldn't say on the air that tobacco companies are mass killers. God knows what they could do to me and Pacifica radio—without the benefit of Ivy League lawyers to advise a payoff.

Saul Landau

Dr. Faust with a French Accent?

January 17, 1996

In 1996, the born-again Dr. Faust celebrated his fifty-second birthday. Since the 1944 Manhattan Project to develop the A-Bomb, he has sought to control the elusive secret of ultimate knowledge (power). He and his minions have detonated thousands of nuclear devices (his word)—two of them over Japanese cities.

The November/December 1995 Bulletin of Atomic Scientists estimated that taxpayers have spent approximately $4 trillion on these "experiments." The late Soviet scientist Andre Sakharov counted some five million cancer and leukemia deaths—the financial and physical equivalent of Faust's soul—which the devil claimed in Goethe's epic.

During World War II, in his new quest for heroic evil, Satan recruited scientists, bureaucrats and generals to undertake the super-secret task because, he told them, Nazi Germany posed an extraordinary threat to western civilization; later it became the eternal Soviet threat, which endured about 45 years.

With the Cold War over, the wily one recruited a new batch of Dr. Fausts, hired by the French government. The ghost of Charles DeGaulle, or a ghost writer for President Chirac, fed the media antiquated lines about France's need for a force de frappe.

What's a few dead fish and some limp plankton, Chirac argued as justification for France's 1995 and 1996 nuclear tests. What's a little inconvenience to South Pacific natives compared with French security? Outraged Australians, Japanese and New Zealanders protested. Tahitians rioted. U.S. and European publics forced their governments to object.

But the U.S. complaint rang hollow. French military planes carrying nuclear equipment gassed up at U.S. airports en route to the South Pacific before the tests. Le Monde's (Sept. 5, 95) Jacques Isuard reported that the U.S. national security apparatus had secretly approved the newest round of French testing as part of the post-Cold War nuclear triumvirate—with England. An

21

Energy Department official said that the French had bought hi-tech nuclear equipment from the U.S. Lawrence Livermore Nuclear Labs. Mike Davis analyzes these facts in a forthcoming issue of *CNS* magazine (*Capitalism, Nature, Socialism*, Volume III, Issue 1, March 1996).

Like the fabled nine-lived cat, the nuclear and unredeemed Dr. Fausts have survived scandals that should have destroyed the Devil's project: zapping soldiers and civilians, for example, to see how humans would respond to whole body radiation; or dropping radioactive waste into the ocean—a process that endured until the early 1970s—because it was convenient. Oh, and the "accidents" at Three Mile Island and Chernobyl. Shudder!

But their explosive experiments continue because governments accept the nuclear gang's line: "it's a dangerous world out there"—a comment first used by Adam and Eve. Next thing you know, Congress will endorse balanced budgets!

I've had enough! How about you? Follow Greenpeace's lead and demand President Clinton end his pact with the nuclear devil, and tell Chirac where to stick his force de frappe.

Saul Landau

Adam and Eve as Drug Addicts?

February 1, 1996

My January Demagogue of the Month award goes to Republican Senator Alfonse D'Amato (NY) and Democrat Dianne Feinstein (CA), co-sponsors of a bill that would require Mexico to cooperate with drug enforcement in order to receive aid. Mexican charlatans labeled the bill imperialism. The White House called it unrealistic. Both missed the point. It's straight-out publicity hunting. Say the word "drugs" and TV space and headlines magically materialize. That's because human beings have always had an ambiguous relationship to mind- and body-altering substances.

We blame drug abuse on producers, shippers and trans-shippers, bankers and money launderers, cops and TV scriptwriters and of course on drug users themselves; or Mother Nature, who made these naughty substances available.

Did Adam and Eve get high? What made them so happy up there, anyway? When you get stoned, you hallucinate and lose your objectivity. Did Eve really meet a talking snake that manipulated her into chomping on the forbidden apple? She must have had a terrible sweet tooth—no Oreos in those days! Only Eros!

Or did Moses actually climb the mountain and see God emerge from a burning bush? What weed do you think was really burning? Then Moses tells a story in which God falls so in love with his prose that everyone has to not only read but obey His dictates.

OK, it's not funny. Thousands die each year from overdoses—legal and illegal drugs. Crack heads and junkies commit crimes for money to feed their habits.

Crime syndicates develop posses and hitmen. Peasants cultivate massive acreage for coca and poppies, instead of for badly-needed grain.

Drugs, legal and illegal, make people sick, lead them to crime, suicide and creativity. But get perspective. Americans adore drugs, yet two hack politicians use the issue to grab headlines by attacking Mexico and diverting the citizenry from more important issues?

Feinstein and D'Amato wouldn't dare threaten to halt block grants to Kentucky, where the killer weed is grown. Tobacco kills thousands more than cocaine, crack and heroine combined. Yet a million black men are serving prison sentences for drug-related offenses.

Let's propose a scenario: a massive police attack destroys networks of suppliers, manufacturers and transshippers. Simultaneously, preventive action inhibits garage labs that would have emerged to replace foreign suppliers. Feinstein and D'Amato celebrate with champagne and cigars. The wealthy get prescriptions from their MDs. Middle class and poor users suffer DTs or commit acts of desperation—or switch to alcohol or new, more addictive tobacco products.

My scenario is as believable as a talking snake seducing a naked woman in a garden. Thanks, Diane and Gus , for inspiring such creativity. Yo drugs!

Saul Landau

Exporting Our Democracy

February 19, 1996

Are you feeling a bit enervated by the current political climate? As Republican hopefuls trade barbs in New Hampshire, Pat Buchanan defends staff members with links to racist groups. Wily Buchanan strategists gloat over having captured the vital undecided bigots vote.

Disgruntled by the baseness, I went into an inside-the-beltway pub and sat next to a National Security apparatchik nursing a malt scotch while reading the *Wall Street Journal*. "Groan," I said, looking at a headline about the amount of money already spent on the primaries.

"This is our brand of political freedom, democracy at its best," he said. "Now, more than ever," my friend boasted, "it should infect the rest of the world. Imagine," he said, longingly, "if Fidel Castro would recognize the unique virtues of our democracy."

"You mean," I said, "Cuba should adopt U.S. style politics?"

"Yes," he replied. "Two parties would materialize, each standing for virtue, the flag and cutting taxes. The U.S. would then lift the embargo. Corporations would set up PACs and lobbies on the island.

"Fidel, like Clinton, a man without a personal fortune, could run for the presidency by marrying a corporate lawyer who would overbill clients and obtain loans from bankers who would collect after the elections. As an opponent, I see one of the ne'er - do-well sons of a leading rum family running on a prostrate tax plan."

"You mean," I said, "one that would leave Cubans a bit flat or flatulent?"

"A former casino owner's son could campaign on prayer in school. Candidates would attack each other's characters viciously at town meetings."

"Sure, and TV spot producers would get wealthy by producing negative advertising," I piped up.

He ignored me. "Candidates would promise to cut government spending, except for the military and police, and they could offer tax relief for the handful of wealthy who would invest their money in Cuban industry and thus provide jobs for the population."

"And abortion," I asked, "which is now legal and easy to obtain?"

"It would resurface as a political issue, along with affirmative action and the sacred right to own firearms. Reporters would thrive, asking candidates about their sex lives and whether they inhaled. Candidates would natter on about mandatory sentences, more prisons and police, less money for health care and schools, where creationism would challenge evolution. Cubans would also have the freedom not to vote; they could spend more time shopping, watching U.S. sitcoms. Another victory over communism." His face was downright beatific.

"You're kidding," I said. "You think the rest of the world would be better off with our system?"

"Better?" he said. "Look at the progress people have made in Russia, Chechnya, Yugoslavia, Nicaragua and those other places that have begun to adopt our ways!"

Saul Landau

Corporate Responsibility

March 30, 1996

Imagine *Newsweek* and the *New York Times* beating up Fortune 500 CEOs? Implying that they've gone too far? And Pat Buchanan as friend of the working stiff?

Even labor leaders who sounded for decades like dyslexic Marxists shouting "workers of the world untie" are finally saying the slogan correctly. The class struggle has begun again and the media have discovered corporate responsibility, a polite euphemism or oxymoron to "neutralize" the devastating effects of downsizing, reducing benefits and moving plants. In the 1940s, business apologists referred to a developing corporate soul—a more poetic, albeit equally inappropriate metaphor to describe the behavior of killer sharks in suits.

Labor Secretary Robert Reich suggested rewarding corporations that adhere to minimum standards of decency. White House aides blasted Reich for raising such a delicate issue at campaign time. Commerce and Treasury bureaucrats simply dismissed Reich as an unrepentant pinko.

But President Clinton didn't desert his old friend Bob—although there are not many of his buddies whom he didn't leave in the lurch when the going got tough. Just think of how a pro-Clinton CEO felt when he heard such anti-corporate blather coming from the bully pulpit itself.

I offer the following apocryphal conversation between a White House staffer and an angry CEO.

CEO: Mention this responsibility crap again and we move our operation to Indonesia. We are responsible to our major stockholders—and our wives and mistresses, of course, who would certainly consider it irresponsible if we didn't earn at least $5 million a year in bonuses.

WH Staffer: Look, we're sorry this issue arose. Blame it on that troublemaker Buchanan. And Bob Reich, a bleeding heart, who saw an opportunity and drove a truck through it. Look at our record. For three years we haven't hinted at corporate wrongdoing—even when you guys downsized by hundreds of thousands of jobs and moved your shops to Mexico. That was after we pushed NAFTA through Congress for you.

CEO: But what have you done for us lately?

WHS: Please, sir, remember who got you GATT and the World Trade Organization; who facilitated the international movement of capital and goods, with tax benefits.

CEO: That was last year. Now we hear how greedy and unpatriotic we are. If not for greed and unpatriotic behavior, we wouldn't be efficient. We fire, I mean lay off unnecessary workers because that is corporate responsibility.

WHS: Occasionally we must refer to national interest, sir.

CEO: Don't wave a flag in my face. My family served in the armed forces for a century—in the quartermaster corps.

As the CEO angrily made for the door, the staffer plaintively called: Please believe me, sir, when the president talks about corporate responsibility he really means the same thing...don't take it amiss...we know who our friends are...don't forget your contribution...

Saul Landau

ABC Live with Regis and Kathy Lee

May 2, 1996

Entertainment Tonight watchers: prepare yourselves for another crushing blow. Kathie Lee Gifford, the day-time chat star who exudes angelic auras, is connected to a Honduran sweat shop operation. Wal-Mart exclusively markets the apparel.

At an April 29 Democratic Policy Committee hearing, labor researchers said that children comprised 10% percent of the Global Fashion Inc. workforce in Choloma, Honduras that manufactured Kathie Lee clothing. The National Labor Committee's Charles Kernaghan testified that teenagers as young as 13 worked fifteen hour shifts, on their feet, in extreme heat.

Often kids work a 75 hour week without overtime pay. Women must raise their hands to receive permission to use a bathroom. They may use the locked lavatories once in the morning and once in the afternoon. They cannot speak to each other during work shifts and undergo searches upon entering the plant lest they bring in snacks that could stain the fabric or impede concentration.

Supervisors scream at the women, "Go faster, faster!" Women who work about an hour to sew a pair of Kathie Lee pants that sell for $20 receive about 25 cents in wages. Should the women protest or organize, the company answers with armed guards who disrupt meetings, threaten violence and of course fire "trouble makers."

Global Fashion work conditions violate Honduran labor laws. But who enforces these laws? Indeed, thousands of similar sweat shops proliferate throughout the third world.

Ask government officials in Honduras or Indonesia and they laugh. Their concern is to lure and keep foreign investors, not enforce labor laws.

At the hearing, a 14-year-old Honduran testified that a Global Fashion supervisor screamed at her, threatened violence and then fired her. She had allegedly looked at papers she was not supposed to see.

Kathie Lee responded to the revelations by crying on her April 30 TV show. "Call me ugly, or untalented," she sobbed, "but don't accuse me of turning my back on children." Kathie Lee donates a few cents from each sale toward children's causes. She and Wal-Mart claim they have now severed connections with Global Fashion.

But Charles Kernaghan says that's not enough. "These women need jobs," he insists "just as U.S. people do. But these jobs must respect internationally recognized human and workers rights." He wants Kathie Lee and Wal-Mart to clean up these conditions, not break with one Honduran sweatshop after they've been caught and then sign on to another in Indonesia.

Congressman George Miller, who chaired the hearing, said the testimony should horrify and enrage people—and give them power to change the way we consume. He said that free trade must become fair trade.

Wipe away those tears, sweat shop Kathie Lee and do something for poor children. And what do you say, Regis?

Saul Landau

Dianna Ortiz

May 7, 1996

A fasting Ursuline Sister gave five weeks of heartburn to the first couple and executive office building residents who had to look at her. Imagine Hillary at a White House dinner gala seeing Sister Dianna's candle outside the dining room window... enough to kill one's appetite for the crab soufflé.

She was kidnapped, raped, tortured, and mutilated by Guatemalan military officials. She claims that an American known as Alejandro ordered her torture stopped and subsequently chauffeured her away from the torture house. Sister Dianna demanded that the U.S. government release classified documents on her case. She ended her five week fast today because of failing health.

"Who was responsible for our life-shattering losses?" she asks. "Who was involved in the hundreds of thousands of disappearances and assassinations carried out by the Guatemalan death squads over the past three decades? What was the role of our own government in these atrocities? We asked because only by learning the truth can we heal and only by learning the truth can we prevent these terrible realities from recurring."

The administration has refused to make thousands of files public—citing national security as its reason. Some officials continue to regard her claims with skepticism. The edited archives she has received from the State Department omit mention of Alejandro. Former Ambassador Thomas Strook described Dianna's rape and torture as a hoax, designed to coincide with congressional hearings about renewing Guatemalan aid. Strook told the *Washington Post* that Dianna had only herself to blame for not trusting embassy personnel after her torture.

What a dilemma! Dianna knew that Guatemalans who received U.S. military equipment, training, and funds were also rapists, torturers and murderers who had massacred tens of thousands of their own mostly indigenous people.

To discover what the thugs did, U.S. officials paid some of them to inform on others. To get "leverage" over thugs, Congress authorized funds to the thugs in 1993. The U.S. gains leverage over the hoodlums that we placed in power by paying them more money. Human rights abuses are resolved by creating relationships with the abusers. Recall that the military official who provided the U.S. Embassy with information on death squads was also the man who organized the 1989 murder of six Jesuit priests.

Late 20th Century imperialist logic demands that informal U.S. colonies accept the facade of law. Back in 1954, the CIA destroyed law in Guatemala. In the 1960s, U.S. Special Forces buried it by converting the Guatemalan military into a modern army—which then attacked, slaughtered and plundered its own people. These were and are our thugs.

Former U.S. Ambassador Strook wonders why Sister Dianna didn't trust him. The embassy staff's very access to information depended on maintaining good relations with her torturers. Skepticism is valuable in the process of discovery. Let's use it on U.S. officials who maintain the facade that Guatemala is a democracy. Why not let Sister Diana see the documents? Is Alejandro a U.S. government employee?

Saul Landau

Arias on Demilitarization

May 16, 1996

Former Costa Rican President Oscar Arias calls for global demilitarization. One's impulse is to laugh.

Arias devised a plan to end Central American wars, for which he received the 1987 Nobel Peace Prize. Thanks to his insistent leadership, and the collapse of the Soviet Union, the Nicaraguan Contras disarmed. The Sandinistas held elections—which they lost. Despite the grim economic picture in Nicaragua, at least mothers no longer fear their that sons will return in body bags. Some 50,000 died in the Contra War.

Peace also came to El Salvador, where perhaps 80,000 died in more than a decade of war. In Guatemala, Arias' plan took hold later and is still in process.

To sell the U.S. establishment on peace in the region, Arias sacrificed Costa Rica's economy by accepting the cruel formulas of the IMF and World Bank. But today Costa Rica still remains better off than its armed neighbors because it doesn't spend on a military. Costa Rica finds it difficult to get into costly wars.

In Africa, Asia, and Latin America, the poorest countries have large militaries, although few of them have ever fought against outside enemies. They kill civilians very well, however.

In 1973, Chile's armed forces destroyed the elected government of Salvador Allende and killed thousands of civilians. Chileans felt secure! Argentina's army killed more of its own people than it did English troops in the Falklands/Malvinas war. But you can't win 'em all. Look at Burundi, Rwanda, Liberia, Burma, Bosnia, Chechen, the Middle East, Sudan, Angola—and you still say they don't need armies?

Each year, the world's nations spend $700 billion on militaries—14 times that spent on development. The developing countries spend 200 billion on their armed forces, just 60 billion less than the United States.

At least Arias didn't tell us to cut the $260 billion defense budget, plus $31 billion more for the CIA. Doesn't Arias know it's a dangerous world? So a billion and a half people live in desperate poverty, have no access to health care, drinking water, or sanitation. At least they have the security of knowing their governments have large armies with modern weapons.

Priorities, President Arias. The Pentagon say it needs every cent—even more, says Congress. The Mexican army needs helicopter gunships to fight narco traffic, the Tutsi must defend against the Hutus and vice versa, the Philippine forces require more modern weapons for something or other.

Arias: Do you really want to stop exciting wars from occurring, deprive young people of opportunities to experience the thrill of modern battle? Do you want soldiers on the unemployment lists? And the tens of thousands who manufacture weapons? Think of their families. Try to sell demilitarization to rational Americans and they'll tell you to go back to peaceful Costa Rica where people must spend lots of time bemoaning the fact that they have no armed forces to be proud of.

Saul Landau

Onion Tears

May 31, 1996

Memorial Day came and went. Memories? Dead young men. Tears? Centuries of wars fought for freedom, democracy, justice. President Clinton, the draft dodger, told us that Memorial Day "is a time to remember what joins us as Americans."

Highways, McDonald's, email? No, he meant death, but not just in war. Ron Brown, a hero, died serving his nation during peacetime—bringing U.S. business people to cash in on rebuilding war-destroyed Bosnia.

Clinton hailed Admiral Jeremy Boorda, who committed suicide in May, presumably also in service to his country? "They are American heroes, too," Clinton said. "We know our country is strong and great today because of them."

No tribute to the slaves upon whose backs the country accumulated wealth, nor tears for the Chinese laborers who built the railroads. Memorial Day memorializes war. U.S. labor waits for September. Remember May Day?

"OK," I said to myself, "let's remember recent wars."

In December, 1941, my first grade teacher explained that the dirty Japs had bombed Pearl Harbor, Hawaii, a U.S. possession. I felt thrilled and indignant over the dastardly act.

During the war years, my teachers taught that in this war for equality one American soldier equaled ten Japs. *My Weekly Reader* featured free China leader Chiang Kai Shek, and avuncular Joe Stalin.

Each Saturday, war movies at the Loewe's 167th Street theater taught that war was fun and necessary. Our side was good, the Axis, unmitigated evil.

"Why don't you enlist?" I asked my father.

He laughed cynically. My cousin was drafted, but luckily served in the Quartermaster Corps. My uncle had pull.

My cousin returned unscathed, unlike millions of others throughout the world. More than 20 million Soviets died. The

Nazis leveled 200 cities. Within two years of the war, Uncle Joe was Stalin the Butcher, our most terrifying enemy.

In 1950, to stop his plan for world conquest, U.S. troops invaded Korea, to defend South Korea, the kind of dictatorship we had fought in World War II. That three-year "police action" cost over a million Korean and Chinese lives, and some 50,000 Americans. The artificial Korean border remained where it had been when the war started. Remember?

Forty years of Cold War. The West fought Soviet surrogates in the periphery. In fact, U.S.-backed British and French armies fought to keep their colonies. Anti-fascist Liberation leaders said "Hey, remember freedom, democracy, independence?" Those were words used by the British and French to recruit them for battle in WWII.

Promise 'em anything—especially in war time. Vietnam! Millions of dead Vietnamese, Laotians, Cambodians and 50,000+ U.S. soldiers. Clinton opposed that war, but does not say on Memorial Day, "I am ashamed of the destruction our military caused." He does not say "let's take steps to end war." No. Keep military budgets high, arms sales brisk and we can shed tears on Memorial Day.

Saul Landau

Israel—Now What?

June 3, 1996

"I grow old, I grow old, I shall wear the bottom of my trousers rolled. Shall I part my hair behind? Do I dare to eat a peach? I shall wear white flannel trousers, and walk upon the beach. I have heard mermaids singing, each to each.

"I do not think that they will sing to me."

Do we become daring after middle age, I ask the dead poet. Do we become boring, predictable—or does excitement still flicker? Does Prufrock relate to Israeli election results, you ask?

Israel, nearly 50 years old, retains narrow, ethnic politics, habits of eternal wars with neighbors and non-Jewish residents, kinky relationships with U.S. politics—a boring, albeit still explosive place.

Binyamin Netanyahu, the right wing Likud candidate, promised peace with security, without Palestinian statehood, without returning the Golan Heights to the treacherous Assad of Syria. He promised to dismantle remaining socialist institutions and let the native Israeli genius unleash itself in the free market. That's what candidate Netanyahu promised. President Netanyahu faces different facts.

Fifty-five percent of Israeli Jews voted for him. Israeli Arabs went for Shimon Peres, although fewer voted—thanks to his murderous pre-election attack on Palestinian refugees in northern Lebanon. A slim margin hardly yields extremist mandates! Yet bitter Peres backers claim that Yigal Amir and his Hamas counterparts won the elections.

Itzhak Rabin's assassin and those who blow up busses on Israeli streets swung votes for Netanyahu. "Oy," said a progressive relative of mine, "now peace is more remote than ever."

I wonder. Charles DeGaulle campaigned as a French nationalist and then granted independence to Algeria. Rabin, the toughest anti-Palestinian, signed the Oslo accords and forced his hand to shake Arafat's in Washington, D.C. in 1993.

The intractable Netanyahu built his anti-terrorist reputation against Hamas tactics, against Palestinian aspirations. Will he now use his right wing aura to continue the peace process that began with the Oslo accords and help unify his divided nation—with U.S. blessings?

The peace agreements benefit Israeli economic and security ambitions. Under its terms, the PLO becomes Israel's surrogate police, Palestinians cede their claims not only to land, but to water as well, a precious commodity in that area.

Netanyahu can use his angry posture as a bargaining tool with Arafat, who could have been suckered by a 3 card monty game.

Prufrock prontificated over the virtues of sex. Netanyahu should not wait "till human voices wake us and we drown" but dive into the sack with the Palestinians and continue the peace process.

Mermaids may sing to Netanyahu. He's had "time to murder." Now is time to "create. Time for all the works and days of hands That lift and drop a question on your plate, Time for you and time for me, And time yet for a hundred indecisions, And for a hundred visions and revisions, Before the taking of a toast and tea."

Saul Landau

Hoover Vacuum Sets the Tone

June 13, 1996

Last week, Hoover Vacuum offered the union a three-tier wage contract. Incoming workers would make $7.50 an hour, the next level would make $9.50, and the top $15.50. For a forty-hour-week, bottom-scale employees would take home less than $10,000 a year; top levels around $23,000.

"If you don't accept the offer," Hoover executives said, "the company will build its new plant in non-union El Paso, Texas." Union officials warned of serious job siphoning from Ohio to Texas, but members of the North Canton, Ohio International Union of Electrical Workers Local overwhelmingly voted to tell the company to shove its offer.

"Throughout the 1980s, we sacrificed for Hoover," one worker said, referring to voluntary pay cuts and waiver of benefits when Hoover faced hard times. Then, in 1986, the Hoover family-owned vacuum company sold the operation. No good deed toward bosses goes unpunished!

Foreign holding companies, the new Hoover owners, sold the rug cleaner factory to Electrolux of Sweden—part of the mergers, buyouts and stock scams that characterize routine dealings in our economy. No longer does Boss Hoover return some profits to the community. Rather, systemic greed prevails. Responsibility means returning profits to stock holders, and more importantly, to corporate execs.

The result, according to the *New York Times*, is that many workers vow to vote this time for Clinton, despite his character problems.

So, if Republicans lose Ohio in '96, they can blame Hoover, a name that reverberates in Republican history—former president Herbert, late FBI Director, J. Edgar.

In 1932, during the Great Depression, a photographer caught President Hoover tossing T-Bones to his dogs while millions of hungry people begged on the streets. Hoover lost the election, as you may recall. The compassionate Franklin Roosevelt told the nation they had nothing to fear but fear itself.

Maybe a slight understatement? But Roosevelt did change capitalism, so that it would survive. He made labor unions part of the new social contract. Despite Roosevelt's sympathy toward working people, however, the police reinforced corporate flanks.

An FBI director who secretly tripped the light fantastic in his living room, clad only in a tutu, persecuted homosexuals and vigilantly investigated labor—for possible red or pink connections, of course. The late FBI tsar showed no mercy toward labor activists who thought workers had rights. He was a lot tougher on activists than he was on Mafia bosses who allegedly had a photo of J. Edgar in tutuland.

So, when I read that the Hoover Vacuum Company had offered workers a choice that could have emanated from the late Herbert or J. Edgar, I ask, "What's in a name?" Class struggle by any other name would rule the day.

Saul Landau

From Watergate to Water White

June 17, 1996

Good Americans must interest themselves in Whitewater—because, says the Republican Senate majority report, Hillary, a corporate lawyer in Little Rock, Arkansas in the 1980s, cooked billing records and on numerous other occasions she and Bill went beyond the windy side of the law. New York Republican Senator Alfonse "Sleazeball" D'Amato also charges that Hillary conveniently misplaced documents and later, after Bill won the election, that she detoured investigations of her friend Vincent Foster's suicide. Off the record, Republican men charge her with dowdy dressing, a large vocabulary, and having thick legs.

To penetrate the shady loans maze and the client overbilling that benefited the Clintons, look to Hillary's ability to convince wealthy friends and partners that playful Billy would become president and that favors done then would yield dividends later. The Clintons' unpaid loans dating from the late 1970s may have helped build a future president's pre-election fund. How else in the 1990s, you should ask, do relatively poor people run for president? Thus, the Clintons owed favors to those who had "lent" them money for more than a decade.

Yet, investigators like D'Amato and House leader Newt Gingrich have waded in tainted money over the past two years. Republican attempts to use Whitewater to smear the Clintons thus gives opportunism a bad name. Yes, Whitewater reveals unsavory Clinton dealings on many levels, but why pick on Hillary?

Clinton-hating fundamentalists see high-powered lawyer Hillary as a defender of the profane: women's rights.

Some of these Republicans still think loading the dishwasher means getting their wives drunk. Twenty three years ago during Watergate, no one cried "Cherchez la femme, for Pat Nixon." Or blamed George and Ron's foibles on Barbara or Nancy. When Carter faced credibility problems, did Republicans attack Roselynne? Did Betty Ford suffer insult because her husband couldn't simultaneously walk and chew gum? Did Lady Bird take the rap for Lyndon on Vietnam, or Jackie Jack's mistake at the Bay of Pigs? Did Mamie get blasted when Ike's aide took a fur coat from a lobbyist? Who would've thought of slandering Bess Truman for Harry's goofs?

Eleanor Roosevelt, however,—there's a precedent. Westbrook Pegler, the 1940s print media Rush Limbaugh, called her *la boca grande*. Pundits hated her outspoken liberalism, her activism for Negro and women's rights. I remember Eleanor and Hillary is no Eleanor. Hillary, an educated Heidi Fleiss, turned legal tricks, and brought money home so her man could become president—since women can't yet aspire for the job.

FDR believed that if you make serious enemies among the minority, it means that your policies benefit the majority. The patrician Roosevelts didn't need shady loans or overbilling for campaign finance. Whitewater has come to mean corruption in the White House: FBI files, travel hanky panky, sexual ambition—and money-grubbing and trading for favors above all. If Whitewater teaches us a lesson, it's that campaign financing reform's time has come. How do we teach this to Congress?

Saul Landau

Southern Baptists to Convert Jews

June 18, 1996

I'm leaving Katz's delicatessen on Houston Street in New York, where they had a sign that said "Send a Katz's salami to your boy in the army," when a finger taps me on the shoulder.

"Are you a member of the Hebrew faith, suh?"

The guy's wearing a cheap suit, a Woolworth tie and a marine haircut. He has a ratty bible in one hand and leaflets in the other.

"Beat it," I say.

"Jesus awaits you, my friend," he tells me.

"You got the wrong guy," I tell him. "I'm not your friend and 'Hebrew faith' is an anti-Semite's way of saying I'm Jewish. Peddle your papers where people will buy them."

"No, suh," he replied. "I'm a Southern Baptist and my elders have decided that our mission is to bring people who look like you—or sound or smell or walk or whatever like you—to the revealed word of Jesus Christ."

This is a joke, I tell myself. My friends are filming this for *America's Funniest Home Videos*.

I see in his missionary eyes reflections of burning crosses in front of black churches, Cossacks spearing babies, Nazis rounding up Jews. I see pudgy Pat Roberston unctuously hustling money on TV, Ralph Reed and his Christian Coalition army killing abortion doctors, I see Jimmy Swaggert mishandling an underage hooker.

He hands me a flyer that says: "Jews convert. You need not burn in the hottest of all hells. Repent! Convert! You can be saved!"

"Is this some fraternity initiation?" I ask him.

"Suh," he says, serious as a Sunday school teacher sagely suggesting that only abstinence can assure sinners of true salvation, "see the light of Christ, bask in the glow of the Holy Ghost and reap the benefits of baptism. You cannot understand jubilation until your head has been immersed in Jordan's purifying waters."

"Let me ask you something," I said to him, trying to retain my calm. "You ever been to Coney Island? Do you know drek from Kosherer foddem? You know any Jews?"

"Suh, in the Mississippi town where I was raised, a family of Hebrew inclination ran the General Store and reputedly amassed fabulous wealth thanks to their niggardly ways."

"Their what?"

"Stingy, suh, miserly, hesitant to part with post-confederate money, if you get my drift."

"You sound like an anti-Semite," I told him.

"I'm no anti-Semite, suh. In my home town, anti-Semites are people who hate Jews more than they're supposed to. Save your wretched soul, suh. If you convert, my missionary career will advance in the eyes of God and of the Church elders who have dispatched thousands of us."

"Not today," I concluded. "Good luck. You'll need it," I said, taking his leaflet. "I hope they don't send you to Iran after you fail at this job."

Saul Landau

Democracy versus Drug Money

July 12, 1996

No good deed goes unpunished! Noble efforts to spread our democratic system to Latin America have led directly to a dilemma—drug cartels contribute to electoral campaigns.

We exported our fabulous election system to less enlightened countries, thus bringing modern television campaign spots into people's living rooms, or huts. But this of course makes campaigning more expensive.

In Bolivia, Columbia or even Mexico, special interests donate tens of millions of dollars to elect friendly candidates. In 1994, the Governor of Tabasco spent $70 million to win his election. Cynics suspect drug money bought the election. In the United States, legitimate private sector donors like alcohol, tobacco and pharmaceutical companies donate fortunes and expect the winners to respond favorably to their interests.

Clinton reminded Boris Yeltsin to keep buying U.S. chickens, but that couldn't have been related to Tyson's Chicken Company in Arkansas contributing to Bill's campaign. Our democracy means one dollar, one vote, er, I mean, one man or, er, woman, or even black person... Well, you get the idea. Money buys votes.

In the absence of large legal businesses in some Latin American countries, drug cartels contribute the lion's share of campaign money. They contributed heavily to Ernesto Samper's recent election in Colombia, and Jaime Paz Zamora's victory in Bolivia in 1989.

Under our great system, the campaigner must hire U.S. consultants who then launch expensive TV and billboard advertising campaigns. These tactics defuse issues and focus political debate on images, where it belongs, rather than on mere substance. Consultants hold fundraising dinners. At one such affair, hosted by former Mexican president Carlos Salinas de Gortari, several participants contributed $25 million each to ruling party coffers.

Do you think the contributors received any favors for their largesse?

But faced with solid evidence of cartel money going to Samper's campaign, what choice did Clinton have but to revoke his visa? Ah, the drug war dilemma. In Bolivia, in 1989, we feared that revoking the visa of an elected narco official would destabilize the fragile democracy that we had fostered by exporting our costly election system.

Samper's case arose at election time. The man who didn't inhale could hardly afford a soft-on-drugs image. Drug cartels sell their unsavory products to unsuspecting American consumers—with the idea of addicting them. Cynics say that such marketing techniques originated with tobacco companies, but I've never seen crack sellers giving their product away on street corners; nor billboards telling me that cocaine means you've come a long way or gives Newport pleasure. But I digress.

In Cold War days, the Pentagon paid Latin American militaries. They still pay them, now that we have successfully encouraged free marketing of elections. The one with the most money wins. Isn't that the essence of free market?

Saul Landau

The Olympics

July 16, 1996

Goethe wrote about Heaven, "The indescribable. Here it is done." TV viewers on earth await the vicarious experiences that prove "Earth's sufficency"—at least in sports. The great human gene pool exhibits its ever more agile, stronger, faster specimens—thanks to Coca Cola. What "progress" we've made.

Imagine Mercury, the god of speed, competing against Michael Johnson. In those days, no one ran the hundred yard dash in under 10 seconds. The contemporary javelin and hammer throwers would have humbled the old gods. Neptune himself might have lagged behind modern swimmers. Oh, but you may as well try and catch the wind. Buy Nikes!

Imagine Olympus' best going against the Dream Team, or vying with contemporary jumpers and vaulters. Our athletes accomplish their feats without the aid of steroids. Did the Greek gods use muscle-expanding substances? No urine tests in those days.

Legend has the gods drinking nectar. Today's athletes drink Coca Cola. Indeed, Coke has become inseparable from the Olympic Games. Billboards claim it as the Olympic drink. Singing and dancing commercials celebrate youth, beauty, strength and endurance and link these attributes with refreshing Coca Cola.

How come we don't barf? The idea of attaching to Olympic competition a high-caloric, overly-sweet, hard-to-digest, addictive bubble water loaded with chemical substances that remove paint from cars and should appear in urine tests!

Don't forget Nike and Adidas, manufacturers of infinite varieties of running, jumping and walking shoes, shorts, t-shirts, running suits and other sports paraphernalia.

They pay Michael Jordan $25 million dollars to endorse sneakers so that idolizing kids will buy the basketball shoes he wears. Nikes can cost over $125, quite a sum for poor kids to pay. Some have murdered to get them.

Workers who make these articles earn less than 50 cents an hour. What would Zeus say to such behavior on the part of crass mortals? Would he chastise Jordan, the descendent of slaves, who has risen to multi millionaire status? The American public that pays lots of money to watch him perform? What the public wants, it gets, say the corporate sponsors. "In veins of mountains, under building-bases, coined and uncoined, there's gold in many places," said Mephistopheles.

Would the gods punish the corrupters of virtue, the corporate CEOs that luxuriate in profits made from the peddling of human flesh?

The Olympic Games, once the pinnacle of performance as virtue, truth, beauty! Some athletes have rescued the Games from commercial avarice and narrow nationalism. Jim Thorpe and Jesse Owens won medals that symbolized their peoples' unrealized potential. In 1968, African-American speedsters held up clenched fists to challenge U.S. segregation at the Olympic victory ceremonies in Mexico City.

The Atlanta corporate elite prepare for a massive shopping spree—the real purpose of contemporary Olympic Games. But, why should we expect sports to rise above the rest of modern life?

Saul Landau

Virtual versus Real New World Order

October 1, 1996

The papers and TV present dreary news and stimulating ads. Yes, the new century promises to produce order and happiness—if you can afford to protect yourself from the growing dangers to your wealth.

Security once meant a thumb and a blanket. Now security means the affluent hiring guards with weapons, the government tapping phones, opening other people's mail, subjecting colored people to searches, evicting aliens. The propertied classes resort to internal passport systems at their apartment and office buildings. Police dogs sniff suspicious-looking characters in public places. TV cameras and monitors are everywhere. George Orwell's *1984*, Aldous Huxley's *Brave New World*?

No. It's the sci-fi 21st century. Virtual Security! Virtual happiness! Medical technology promises the rich practically endless life—for a price. Each multi millionaire can buy his own MRI and a staff of medical specialists. He will stock his refrigerator with reserve organs and blood supplies—all well tested. His mansion basement will contain spare limbs, hips and elbows—to replace the used ones. *Cocoon*?

The minority that retains access to the global mall will experience shopping as unfathomable peaks of ecstasy. The global shopping network will induce consumers to dream about a product, record the dream digitally and have the product delivered when the wishful shopper awakens—with a 30-day trial period, of course.

Compare this virtual perspective for the best and richest with a smattering of current grim headlines. The new world order falls a bit short of imposing its novel forms on "those people." Washington supports the Taliban Afghan rebels because they will create order in that war-wrecked nation. Upon entering Kabul, the capital, the order-making rebels hung the previous rulers. Didn't the CIA destabilize Afghanistan some years ago? Memory dims—each time we turn on the TV.

A South African cop admits that one of his buddies whacked Swedish Prime Minister Olaf Palme in Stockholm in 1986. The killers want amnesty—only following orders. Remember? No? Not to worry. The black and white channel occasionally reruns *Judgment at Nuremberg*.

Netanyahu and Arafat? Tired old arguments from a family sitcom where brothers fight about who owns the family land, and over rights to control parts of the house with one liners like "I opened a tunnel into your church so tourists could see how ridiculous you look praying" and "besides that, the land belongs to me, not you." Ha Ha! goes the canned laugh track. "And you deserve to be shot." Ho Ho!

"Why did you open the tunnel without telling the person who hates you most? And at midnight? You want peace, how about a piece of my fist?" Ha Ha!

Well, what do you want—more Netanyahu versus Arafat, revelations of CIA drug dealing to LA gangs, apartheid murderers, presidential debates? Or the delicious possibility of eternal shopping, to satisfy each new need with new commodities, produced in sweatshops?

Saul Landau

Spit Happens

October 7, 1996

Roberto Alomar, Baltimore Orioles second baseman, spit in umpire John Hirschbeck's face. Hirschbeck, you remember, called a ball a strike and tossed the protesting Alomar out of a late-season game. Alomar then commented that the umpire had grown bitter after his son had died from a rare disease.

Even Alomar's boyish team mates condemned such behavior as immature. I say Alomar had mitigating circumstances. Hirschbeck's bad call could've cost Baltimore a playoff berth which, in turn, would cost Alomar, each Oriole and the owner tens of thousands of extra dollars.

Does a relatively low-paid ump have the right to toss a millionaire ball player? Fans pay $20 to watch Alomar homer or make sparkling defensive plays. And this nobody ump throws him out of the game! No wonder Robbie got spitting mad.

In the 90s—like the 80s and 70s—winning isn't everything, as the guru Vince Lombardi taught, it's the only thing. Corporate CEOs toss tens of thousands of families into material hell by laying them off—to improve company profits and earn themselves juicy bonuses. The laid-off workers didn't make bad calls on the CEO at the company softball game, or make nasty remarks about his kids. He did it because the economic laws of his life demand it.

Landlords kick families into the streets for nonpayment of rent. Terrible, we mutter in sympathy, but the law's the law. The rich have rights—to protect what they acquired, no matter how they got it.

Well-paid members of Congress and the even-better-paid president of the United States who have taken tens of millions from greedy special interests denied minimal survival funds to the poorest people. Too bad. Let 'em work for a living. How about the welfare recipients who descended from slaves who never received a penny for their labor? That's history!

The new cultural message says that only wealth and winning matter. Ghetto and barrio kids kill for fancy jackets or designer sneakers so they can emulate Michael Jordan or Robbie Alomar—that's what the commercials tell them.

Alomar enjoys high prestige because he's rich and famous. A bad call could cost him money and victory. And TV teaches us that we should expect a violent reaction from him.

Baseball is a game, you say? Players are role models for millions of little leaguers who learn sportsmanship and discipline? Have you watched parents screaming at Little League umps, cursing their kids' coaches and the kids themselves for making errors? Baseball is business. In business, the rich don't pay for abusing the poor.

Anyway, the Orioles made the American League finals and Hirschbeck and Alomar have reconciled. Do you think Robbie and the Orioles paid the poor ump under the table?

Moral: Millionaire players can orally ejaculate in an ump's face and still play ball. Yep, it's the 90s, and spit happens!

Saul Landau

Pardonez Moi?

October 8, 1996

The Republicans want Whitewater Special Prosecutor Kenneth Starr to put Clinton Democrats in prison. Clinton staffers apparently searched FBI files to find incriminating material on Republicans. Is this 19th Century Russia where a politician predicted that if they ever got a two-party system one party would be in office, the other in prison?

Starr lacks material for high-level indictments before the Congressional elections, but Republican revenge-seekers hope that if Clinton wins, the Special Prosecutor will make him the first president to ride in a Chief Exec's limo with license plates made by the first lady.

Indeed, Bob Dole has made the mere possibility that Bill Clinton might pardon his former Whitewater buddies into a campaign issue. Dole has called upon the president to swear he will not issue pardons.

This rings hollow. Ask yourself—if Dole truly cared about justice in the Whitewater affair, would he demand that Clinton promise not to pardon former Clinton business partners James or Susan MacDougall, or former Arkansas governor Jim Guy Tucker? Ask gay activists, environmentalists or people Clinton said he'd put first about the value of his pledges.

Second, consistency! Does Dole recall that he led the fight to get President George Bush to pardon Caspar Weinberger, former Defense Secretary, and five other top Republican officials indicted in the Iran Contra scandal? Lawrence Walsh, former Special Prosecutor in that affair, has devoted two chapters of his forthcoming book, *Firewall*, to the pardon episode.

Dole's priorities, Walsh reports, seem to go more toward attempting "to exploit President Clinton's connection with long-ago business transactions that ended before he became president." The same Bob Dole demanded "pardons for crimes of constitutional dimension committed in office by a Reagan Cabinet officer."

Anyway, what's more important, a little violation of the Constitution or truly evil savings and loan schemes? Well, that's the question if you're a Democrat. Bob Dole thought Special Prosecutor Walsh collaborated with the Democrats when he indicted upstanding Republicans like Cappy Weinberger and Ollie North.

The Democrats think Starr works for the Republican National Committee, trying to smear the Clintons sufficiently to win votes for Dole. Hey, Bob, remember, Gerald Ford pardoned Richard Nixon. And a good thing too. Nixon emerged from under the cloud of indictment and turned into a man the elite asked for advice. As Nixon's transformation from criminal to statesman showed, pardons change character—or at least the image of character.

If Aaron Burr had pardoned Alexander Hamilton instead of shooting him in a duel, our history could have been different. Who knows? Jim Guy Tucker might become president of the United States, if he gets out of prison. So just remember, Bob, the wise man thinks once before he speaks twice—as a Chinese proverb probably said.

Saul Landau

The CIA Strikes Again

October 17, 1996

Test your memory! 1950s: CIA experiments with drugs, people commit suicide, it overthrows democratic governments in Iran, Guatemala. 1960s: CIA assassination squads, Vietnam, Phoenix Program. 1996: old bad deeds convert to new scandals.

The CIA is accused of coddling drug dealers who introduced crack into the Los Angeles ghettos during the 1980s Contra war. In the 1990s, the Agency employed Emanuel Constant, Haitian death squad leader. CIA-agent Constant allegedly helped plan the 1993 murder of Guy Malary, Haitian Justice Minister. Then the U.S. government released Constant after the Haitian government demanded his deportation. He had a few good CIA stories to tell.

Shocked? What's the lesson? That when we undertook the mission of saving the world from Godless communism we needed an agency able to step beyond the narrow boundaries of the Ten Commandments and do what had to be done. Our mission was heroic, even if we can't define it clearly.

Heroic means good; or can heroic also involve evil? Like Hitler's quest for world conquest. The United States built an empire, but the imperial road is inevitably paved with corpses. Sometimes, we taxpayers have to confront that we, through the guise of the CIA, authorize and finance murder.

We think of ourselves as citizens of a republic with accountable institutions, not an empire. The scandals, however, force us to see the contradictions. We live in tension with an imperial apparatus that purports to protect our national security, which classified and top secret, cannot be defined.

The current scandal arose when the Center for Constitutional Rights filed a law suit against Emanuel Constant and released documents that connected him with the CIA—to which he provided information for $500 a month. In other words, Constant told the CIA about killings, torture and mayhem carried out by his organization, FRAPH, Front for Advancement and

Progress in Haiti. Did the CIA analyze this data for policy making? Isn't that what intelligence agencies are supposed to do? Hire murderers to tell them when and whom they are going to kill and then policy results?

In 1991, right wing Haitian military and police thugs overthrew President Aristide and his government. The U.S. government tsk-tsked their disapproval while coddling the military usurpers and running disinformation against Aristide.

Citizens will be happier not knowing about Constant and other unpleasant clandestine operations. Successful CIA coups can mean we don't have to intervene with troops. So what if they're incompatible with republican principles? It's not always clean work saving the world and fighting the communist, er, I mean terrorist, narco-trafficking, rogue state enemies.

We live in the world's strongest and toughest empire. Occasionally, imperial officials get caught in embarrassing situations, like keeping murderers on payroll. A small price to pay for world power, they claim when caught!

When citizens reveal CIA dirty deeds, they strengthen the republic and weaken the empire. You like the sound of the CIA on the defensive? Hail to the Center for Constitutional Rights.

Saul Landau

Ah, the Virtues of Conspiracy

October 21, 1996

Some listeners berate me for paying insufficient attention to conspiracies. I admit that government and corporate plotting exist, but, I maintain, the objectives of such cabals are often downright silly, albeit evil, and the conspirators rarely calculate the downside.

Richard Nixon, for example, conspired to cover up the 1972 Watergate break-in. But Tricky Dick's money insecurity prevailed. He refused to destroy the tapes that ultimately led to his undoing. The publisher had warned him that without the tapes, his presidential memoirs merited a smaller advance.

Nixon, without thinking twice, ordered the CIA to conspire to overthrow the Salvador Allende government in Chile. Nixon compiled a secret enemies list on whom he sicced the FBI and the IRS. In November 1963, just before the Kennedy assassination, Nixon was in Dallas. Nixon hated Kennedy, had mafia ties and close relations with CIA and anti-Castro Cuban spooks that assassination mavens have linked to the fatal plot; ergo, Nixon was part of the Kennedy assassination.

That's OK for movies. In Oliver Stone's *JFK*, the character of Colonel Fletcher Prouty, played by Donald Sutherland, implicates the entire national security apparatus right up through LBJ in the Kennedy shooting. Nothing wrong with this—as long as you're making a thriller.

All this prefaces a recent conversation at a Washington reception. A journalist asked a senior national security official why Clinton signed the Helms-Burton bill, which codified the U.S. embargo on Cuba, thus tying the president's hands should he want to subsequently lift the embargo.

"We didn't pay enough attention to Cuba," he said. "We didn't realize the implications. The Cubans shot down the planes." He referred to the February downing of two light planes flown by the anti-Castro Brothers to the Rescue over or near

57

Cuban airspace. "We responded too impulsively," he shrugged. "We should've paid more attention to details."

There's more! The official in charge of Cuba policy had resigned three weeks before the downing of the planes. He had requested the FAA to revoke Brothers to the Rescue pilots' licenses. The FAA had not complied. Perhaps, an official suggested, because the Miami FAA chief feared that volatile Cuban exiles would bomb his house.

Such quirks don't fit conspiracy theories. Yet, the unpredictable regularly happens—like catching a cold or having your car radio stolen.

So, conspiracy buffs, write scripts about how events ought to have happened. Occasionally, conspiracies work and historical tragedies result that change human destiny, like the assassination in Dallas or the coup in Chile.

Don't underestimate the banality factor, the stupidity element and most prevalent, the irresponsibility dimension. As the official said in retrospect on Cuba policy, "we should've paid more attention." Had he conspired he might've had clearer focus.

Saul Landau

A New and Optimistic Poll

October 22, 1996

Political aspirants poll the American public to discover how this amorphous entity feels about practically everything. Thus, we learn from the mass media and the mostly right-wing talk show hosts that the public loves the military, trusts the corporation and hates big government and big labor, demands cut backs on programs for the poor and thinks environmentalists are kooks who take jobs away from workers.

But, a recent survey taken by the Pew Research Center for the People and the Press shows that the public appears far more ambivalent than the media or mainstream politicians allow. In fact, despite the incessant barrage of corporate propaganda to convince Americans that the more greedy the corporations become, the better the health of our nation, the public doesn't buy it.

Quite the contrary. A substantial majority of those polled, including Republicans, believed it unhealthy to have vast concentration of wealth in corporate hands. Most interviewed said corporations made excessive profits.

Similarly, voters felt strongly that the government should protect the environment and although overwhelmingly in favor of a strong defense, thought less should be spent on the military. While the majority favored reform of existing welfare structures, they also felt government needed to do more to help the poor.

If this study correctly reflects public opinion, how do we explain the prevailing media and political axioms that have the public supporting just the opposite points of view?

Indeed, even sectors of the left have accepted the glib myths offered by mainstream media and the political hacks who front for bond dealers and corporate giants. I'm referring here to Clinton, Dole, Gingrich and many of the congressional Democrats who routinely vote as if their make-believe free market world was the real one.

If the Pew Study accurately reflects political thought—and there's no reason to believe otherwise, from my conversations with people all over the country—then it's time to stop wringing our collective hands in despair over the public's apathy or stupidity and to begin sending hard-hitting truth squads out to clarify issues.

When Clinton tells us how the welfare bill offered great opportunities for the poor, we shouldn't just wait for his nose to grow, but reach down deep into our diaphragms and let forth bellowing correctives that will reach the sensors even in his insensitive ears.

When Rush Limbaugh and the other right-wing ranters begin their diatribe, we should get on the phone and confidently tell them they're lying, that they're mouthpieces for corporate greed masquerading as rugged individualists.

As we suffer through pre-election days, noting that Clinton's large lead would allow him to start dating again, let's also prepare ourselves to engage him with an agenda that the Pew Study suggests represents majority thinking.

Hey, by feeling that we represent majority opinion we might begin to have fun again doing politics!

Saul Landau

Election Day Apathy

November 5, 1996

After casting my ballot I felt nauseated. Will I suffer the
moral consequences of voting for people who do not represent
my interests, who give new meaning to the word disappoint-
ment? Be practical, I said to myself. The other guy's worse. I've
always voted for the lesser of two evils, why bitch now?

The nausea abated as I breathed cool autumn air. Outside
the polling center, campaign junkies handed out flyers reminding
voters of their candidates' names. Nearby, several men and
women had outstretched hands.

Stiff them or give each five dollars and get a "bless you"?
Are these people preparing to get thrown off welfare; practicing
their new occupation? Since Democrats revel over the healthy
5.2% unemployment figure, it makes sense for people to beg—
that way they don't cut into the employment roles and with only
several million unemployed, the economy remains robust .

A man stood next to me, waiting for the bus. I assumed by
the sour look on his face that he also had just voted.

"No," he said, "I don't vote. It's a matter of principle."

"What principle?" I demanded.

"I pay taxes," he said. "Therefore, I should be represented,
but neither party, neither candidate represent my interests as a
peace-loving parent and working person. I see Indonesian and
Taiwanese businesses represented. Big oil, gas, cars, insurance,
booze and tobacco buy the supposed people's representatives."

"Wait a second," I stopped him. "Our system may have a
few flaws, but it's still the greatest democracy in the history of
the world. Nations throughout Latin America eagerly copy our
campaign format. As a result tens of millions of people see their
candidates on TV—for a few seconds at a time, except when they
debate, which is too boring to watch. But that's freedom, that's
our way of life."

He stared at me. "I don't look for candidates with charisma,
or that know how to make a speech. I want someone to help

address the difficult issues. Millions of poor will receive no help from either party, either candidate. Millions face insecurity over job loss, which means health care loss. Look how the environment continues to suffer as a result of the perpetual growth and development mystique that has gripped us and which politicians don't question."

He was practically in tears. "Get a hold of yourself," I pleaded. "It's not all that bad. The point is we do have a choice and therefore we have to exercise it."

"No," he countered. "There's little meaningful choice in most of our elections. So I don't vote."

"Citizens have an obligation to vote," I lectured. "If the majority acted like you, what kind of country would we have?"

He smiled. "The majority do act as I do. They don't vote."

"What's your name, Mister," I demanded, as the bus came.

"Joe," he said. "Joe Apathy, but you can call me just plain Joe."

Saul Landau

Don't Call Pinochet a Psychopath!

November 11, 1996

Two Jews face a Nazi firing squad. Before the SS sergeant gives the order to fire, one Jew steps forward. "I have something important to say."

"Be quick about it," the sergeant responds.

"Adolph Hitler is a no good s.o.b," the Jew shouts.

"Why do you have to make trouble?" the other Jew laments.

You won't believe it, but Chileans tell this old joke about Gladys Marin, Chile's communist Party chief, who called Augusto Pinochet a blackmailer and psychopath. When he heard about it, Pinochet filed a court action and, in response, forty cops dragged Mrs. Marin from her car and slammed her into the pokey. And it's all legal. Pinochet, before Chileans voted him out of the presidency in 1990, made it a crime to call the country's leaders nasty names.

I don't want to compare Pinochet to Hitler. Hitler lasted only 12 years in power. Pinochet ruled for 17 and he's still the commander of the armed forces. Pinochet's thugs only killed, tortured and exiled thousands—among them Mrs. Marin's husband, who one day was kidnapped by Pinochet's secret police and never again seen.

OK, Pinochet can't take a joke. But aspiring leaders from different countries worship him. Former Russian strong man Alexander Lebed called him his model. Pinochet demonstrated that 17 years of brutal military rule could convert Chile from democratic socialism into free market democracy.

Before leaving the presidency, Pinochet guaranteed the Chilean military its independence from civilian control. Indeed, Chilean copper sales go directly to support the armed forces. Moreover, Pinochet assured the military four Senate seats, including one for himself after he steps down from command in 1998.

Chile hosts the current Ibero American summit, where all governments except for Cuba are supposedly democratic and practicing free market economics. Other than rapidly growing poverty in most of these countries, the model seems to be working just fine.

Chile's ruling politicians aspire to become the next NAFTA partners and Pinochet flusters them. What will they say to U.S. Congresspeople skeptical of the virtues of these so-called free trade arrangements?

A Spanish court has opened an investigation of Pinochet's links with international terrorism. Americans recall that his agents murdered Orlando Letelier and Ronni Moffitt in Washington in 1976. Spanish lawyers contend that Pinochet ordered the slayings of others of his enemies abroad and of some Spanish citizens in Chile. If he is convicted, the Spanish government would ask for his extradition. How embarrassing!

The ruling Christian Democrat-Socialist coalition tries to dissuade Chileans from raising issues of Pinochet's having institutionalized the military into the nation's political structure. So, the joke returns. Two Chileans face a Pinochet firing squad. Gladys Marin steps forward and says Pinochet is a psychopath. The other Chilean says: "Why do you have to make trouble?" Only he's the just-elected, new president of Chile.

Saul Landau

Texaco, AVIS and Affirmative Action

November 13, 1996

Who needs affirmative action? Racial and gender discrimination are things of the past, claimed supporters of the California "end affirmative action" ballot proposition that passed on election day.

Then—surprise—tapes materialize with voices of Texaco executives referring to African Americans in most ungenerous fashion. Following that, revelations emerge that AVIS Rent-a-Car franchises in the Carolinas discriminate against potential black renters.

Can you imagine, in late 1996, corporate executives still clinging to the glitch of racism from our past? Oh well, like the sexual abuse cases in the army, these minor incidents should not discourage Americans who believe that everyone's equal and therefore no one needs special help in getting jobs or entering institutions of higher learning.

Such an attitude derives from our national view of history—something that once happened, but has little relevance now.

What greater insult can you hurl at someone than "you're history"? With these words bosses fire employees, spouses divorce each other. Clint Eastwood or Arnold Schwartzenegger could use the phrase instead of "make my day" or "hasta la vista, baby."

Millions of students dread history tests fearing they will not retain names, dates and places of our history. Imagine someone saying to them: "you're history!"

The prevailing mood obliterates the past as a factor in the present—at least, for hiring, university placement and other areas where people of color and women had a fleeting chance to compensate for centuries of less-than-equal treatment.

Perhaps it's better to keep history where it belongs, in the national closet under the lock and key of the powerful. That way the public can view historical documents on designated proper occasions.

Admire the Declaration of Independence every July 4th and regret the horrors of slavery during black history month. Such control of the past as relics, to be displayed like museum paintings at certain times, allows Americans to see the present through rose colored glasses that have never been dipped into the great grimy lake of real history.

Without the historical prism with which to view the past, the modern Dr. Pangloss happily relegates race and gender issues to murky antiquity, with other unpleasantness that has occasionally disturbed America's forward trajectory. Indeed, anti-affirmative actionites implicitly deny that events of the past relate to contemporary hiring, school admission or life itself.

What relevance do a couple of centuries of slavery and 100 years of apartheid have on the ability to qualify for jobs or school entrance today? What could exclusion from opportunities to even earn wages for two centuries while producing lots of wealth for others have to do with the current economic position of black people? Absolutely nothing, chant the anti-affirmative actioneers.

As for Texaco and AVIS executives' racist behavior—where could these folks have acquired such attitudes? Surely, the rest of us have overcome the unfortunate parts of our past.

Saul Landau

The CIA and Drugs?

November 17, 1996

The *New York Times*, *Washington Post* and the *Los Angeles Times* suggested that the *San Jose Mercury News* upset the American public for no good reason. *Mercury* reporter Gary Webb broke a story earlier this year alleging that the CIA had connections with crack dealers who sold their product in Los Angeles. Some of the drug sales' profits went to supporting the Nicaraguan Contras, who, you will remember, President Reagan described as the equivalent of our Founding Fathers.

Anyway, the elite newspapers claim Webb and the *Mercury News* irresponsibly exaggerated the CIA role in this drug business and they focused public attention instead on the responsibility of the reporter for getting accurate details. Of course the CIA doesn't make it easy to get details since they keep their records and operations a top secret. This kind of challenge is good for reporters. Anyway, isn't it the establishment press' job to protect the government from the public?

I contacted my own Agency source. We met at a pre-established spot, overlooking the Potomac. He removed his wig, false nose and Groucho Marx mustache and aimed an electronic gadget at me and at the surrounding area to ensure that no one had bugged the place.

"I suppose this is about the CIA dope-dealing scandal in the LA ghetto," he started.

"Yes," I responded. "Did the Agency collaborate with crack dealers who then flooded the LA ghetto with cheap drugs, or did it know nothing about this operation?"

My informant smirked. "Look. We had a job to do. Our mandate dictated that we do anything necessary to protect the free world from the threat of communism. We sent assassins all over the world to kill enemies of freedom. We had a hit list that included Patrice Lumumba, that African red who stirred up trouble in the Congo, and Rafael Trujillo, that no-good Dominican dictator who was stealing from us, and of course the luckiest of all the commies, Fidel Castro. We've tried to bag his butt more times than I can count."

"OK, we knew that, but did the CIA help the LA drug dealers?"

"The CIA staged coups to knock off governments to protect the free world. We wasted the Iranian government in 1953 and put our freedom-loving friend the Shah in power. We got that pinko Arbenz in Guatemala in 1954, that Brazilian wimp in 1964. We've staged covert operations all over the world, paid mercenaries to slaughter thousands. Look at Afghanistan. But it was all done for freedom."

"We know this stuff," I replied, trying to keep him on the point. "Did the Agency consort with drug dealers in the USA?"

"We've assassinated, subverted, overthrown, destabilized, slaughtered and altered other peoples' destinies all over the world, and I approve of those actions. But dealing drugs? Please, there are some things that we wouldn't do even for the great cause of freedom. "

"But," he added, "maybe not all the CIA operatives were as moral as I am."

Saul Landau

Castro and the Pope

November 29, 1996

Newspaper front pages throughout the world featured a photo of Fidel Castro, age 70, and the pope, 76, conversing at the Vatican. No reporters attended the session, after which the pope accepted Castro's invitation to visit Cuba next year.

Speculation abounded. Would Castro allow the church in Cuba more freedom as a pre condition for the Pontiff's visit? Shortly after the revolution, Fidel cracked down and expelled hundreds of foreign priests, whom he accused of fomenting counter revolution.

Would Castro offer to allow them to return?

I, too, was curious. So I phoned my close friend who brushes the lint from the pope's robes to find out what they actually said. Here's his account.

CASTRO: Do I have to kiss your ring? There's no photographer around?

POPE: Go ahead and kiss it. I won't tell anyone. But if you don't, I'll tell everyone you did.

CASTRO (kisses pope's ring): Your hand stinks. Did you chop your own garlic for lunch? What did you have for lunch anyway?

POPE: Kielbasa. It's Polish sausage. You want some? I have a little left over in my robe pocket.

CASTRO: I'll pass, thanks. Let's get down to business. I want you to come to Cuba, which will contribute to my government's prestige and help build peace. In return, the Church can do what it wants—within reason.

POPE: Look, Fidel, can I call you by your first name? OK. Sure, I'll visit Cuba, make all those signs with my hands, talk about peace and reconciliation, bless thousands of crying women and innocent children, denounce the Helms-Burton bill, criticize your government for violating human rights and I'll even visit the AIDS clinics.

CASTRO: I would expect nothing less.

POPE: But I wanted to see you for a different reason. What plans do you have for retiring?

CASTRO: You know I can't retire until the United States lifts the embargo. That might not occur until the year 2080.

POPE: OK, then in 2081, I want you to succeed me as pope. I'm a few years older than you and by that time I'll be ready to hang up my hat, or robes.

CASTRO: I'm honored, Your Holiness. Can I call you that? I've been thinking about what to do when I retire, aside from writing my memoirs, but being pope…that would be a challenge. You know, I've grown bored facing one silly American president after another. But how could you propose a non-believer like me, who is even pro-choice?

POPE: I knew you'd be interested. You're the kind of guy who can put real spark into the church, spread the doctrine to atheists and heathens everywhere. You give good TV and that's what counts these days.

CASTRO: But I'm Cuban. Would the cardinals accept another non-Italian?

POPE: Sure, they're hopelessly divided. You know how they chose me? They couldn't agree on any candidate, so they took a Pole (poll)!

Saul Landau

TV Is Virtually Life Itself

December 2, 1996

I've had it with TV. My ten-year-old consented to eat breakfast this Sunday only after I threatened to turn off the set. Of course, I brought her eggs into the TV room so she could watch the exciting climax of a cartoon bird obliterating a 'toon cat.

The X Files, her favorite show, goes on later. "Huh huh, huh, huh," she imitates Beavis or Butthead. Don't these shows frighten you? "That's the whole idea, Dad. Take a chill pill. Stop spazzing."

My teenage daughter does her homework while watching Beverly Hills 90 thousand something. "How can I do this boring homework unless I'm distracted?" she explains.

My wife goes to sleep with TV on. "White noise," she tells me.

I watch political talk shows on weekends, *Nightline* and important athletic events. Once in a while, I'll catch *ER* or *Homicide*. "Don't feel guilty," I tell myself, "TV's here to stay." Each year, peace-loving Americans watch thousands of violent hours. By 2020 we'll watch 119 hours more yearly than we watched in 1996, a new study reports.

We're an obedient people. TV commands us to watch. Don't cook, have sex, read, see your friends and neighbors and especially don't get active in politics, which will take you away from TV four or more nights a week.

What greater pleasure than spending productive evenings watching TV? Have a drink, avoid family fights and the risks of associating with other people, which can lead to amorous or business involvements—or dangerous endeavors like friendship.

TV is safe—and best of all it directs your needs outside of your family and friendship circles. It tells you to go to the store or the phone and buy something—but only for the purpose of improving your life. You can lose weight, purchase a status symbol that promises to give you a better sex life and more respect—and even more power rounding the curves. Moreover,

71

when you shop, you also help the economy. You can feel patriotic, if not downright virtuous.

Next to the automobile, television has done more to shape our civilization than any other technology, even the atom bomb. You can enjoy a virtual life of images that will induce far greater bliss than real people can give you with all their problems. Select from the porn channels, the shopping channels, the sports and religion channels. With new high definition technology, TV experience outdoes even a good acid trip. Surrogate sex! Vicarious violence! In vivid color and Dolby stereo!

During this prolonged holiday period, malls may stay open 24 hours a day. Visit your nearest all purpose store!

This message was sponsored by the television programmers of America in conjunction with the Promote Mental Health Association.

"Hey, kid, put that knife down! That's not how you treat your little sister!"

Saul Landau

A Balanced Budget Gives Comfort

December 9, 1996

My mother taught me not to spend more than I earned because overspending inevitably led to borrowing. For emphasis, she quoted Shakespeare: "Neither a borrower nor a lender be." Later, I learned that Shakespeare had put those words into the mouth of Polonius, a pompous jerk who recited old saws and missed the point—except of Hamlet's sword, which got him in the belly. My mother also advised me to stash money—for the future.

What's this got to do with balancing the national budget, an idea that comforts many Americans? Their parents, like mine, recited financial-management clichés from Shakespeare and from Ben Franklin. "A penny saved is a penny earned!" This wisdom belonged to the pre-credit card era. If Americans today stopped borrowing and lending and saved their pennies, the economy would collapse in a month. Imagine the 1996 U.S. budget run on Franklin's formula!

But Ronald Reagan's scriptwriters understood that we derive solace from hearing those old maxims and they inserted them into the president's speeches. Reagan's recital of banalities helped disguise the fact that he had invested fortunes on weapons systems to protect us from the evil enemy that he said had grown militarily stronger and more threatening to God and western civilization.

So, Reagan turned U.S. economic planning over to the military while lecturing the public on the virtues of a balanced budget—and on the evils of big government, which he made bigger by spending without raising taxes to pay for his military largesse.

Next to communism and the Sandinistas, you recall, Reagan considered taxes the world's worst enemy and he cut them, just as he demanded money for Star Wars and other fantastic toys.

Then, someone told Reagan that government spending had gotten out of control. He couldn't cut the military budget that

God had ordered increased, but the poor—well, they'd been feeding at the public trough since he could remember and perhaps the time had come to cut them off.

"Sure," his advisers whispered in his ear, "the poor have had their fair chance and they've blown it."

Thus, from the bully pulpit, Reagan set the context of modern debate. Balance the budget by taking from the poor.

Enter Bill Clinton, saying he'd put people first. He meant government should invest for future generations' education and other basic needs.

But when his advisers ran this notion up the proverbial flagpole, not enough voters or corporate executives saluted. And the Clintons, having matured since the days when they took those frivolous Whitewater loans, have now swung firmly toward a balanced budget. But the election is over. Why couldn't Clinton balance the budget by cutting military spending, so at least some of the public's money gets spent on the public instead of on subsidies for corporate benefits? Just to restore a little balance? Surely, Ben Franklin and Shakespeare—well, Polonius would have approved!

Saul Landau

Restoring Democracy in Cuba

December 13, 1996

When President Clinton signed the Helms-Burton bill, he forged a link in the continuity of presidents who have tried to bring "democracy" to Cuba. Back in the 1790s, John Adams hoped to make the island part of our democracy by annexing it. President Buchanan thought Cuba would be a perfect state—a slave state. Unfortunately, the North wouldn't agree without getting an equivalent free state. After Civil War broke out we waited until 1898, when President McKinley sent U.S. forces to Cuba to help Cubans struggle for independence against Spain. The Cubans forgot to ask for our help, but we helped anyway by occupying her territory. As a gesture of democratic good will, we even built a naval base on Cuban soil.

As soon as Cuba elected its first president with our supervision, we left, as we said we would. We were forced to return soon after in 1909 to suppress a rebellion there that endangered U.S. property, the very core of our democracy.

Interventions build character in any case, and Cuban presidents always welcomed investors who introduced subtle varieties of our democracy—for example, through casinos run by colorful Americans of Italian descent. In 1959, bearded, long-haired Cubans staged a revolution, without receiving our permission.

So, to restore democracy, President Kennedy authorized a CIA-backed Cuban exile force to invade the island. The CIA selected brigade members from propertied families trying to reclaim their holdings—a key to the democratic process.

Over the years, U.S. presidents committed to democracy in Cuba sent in assassins and saboteurs and imposed an embargo on the disobedient island. Some questioned this method of teaching democracy, but not the goal itself. After all, the Castro government had committed the ultimate no-no by inviting the evil Soviet reds into our hemisphere.

In 1992, with those naughty Soviets where they belonged, our Congress and president designed a new pedagogy for Cuba—reward and punishment. If the Cuban government cooperated and allowed us to subvert its system, we would reward them in unspecified ways. To prove our sincerity, we even called this bill The Cuba Democracy Act.

The method worked. Tens of thousands of Cubans sailed or floated to the United States. Unfortunately, we hadn't prepared to receive so many democracy-seeking foreigners arriving in Florida on inner tubes. Indeed, the massive exodus showed that our policy was too successful for our own good. Some Members of Congress invented yet a new pedagogy.

The Cuban Liberty Act or Helms-Burton Act aims to revive democracy in Cuba through law suits. Former large Cuban property owners by suing in U.S. courts will get damages on property confiscated from them by the revolution. Litigious behavior is so American and it will punish Cuba and those who invest there—as well as inhibit potential investors. Thus we teach democratic lessons to the whole world—in case anyone should doubt the depth of our commitment to democracy in Cuba.

Saul Landau

The New Cabinet

December 14, 1996

The new Cabinet appointments, I thought, would offer a clue about Clinton's second term agenda.

So, I asked my White House source what Madeline Albright's appointment at State meant.

"Pay-off to women for voting for Clinton. But I don't think she would have gotten the job if Christopher was still alive," he joked.

"Seriously," he continued, "this woman will show the flag with her mouth to win the final battles of the Cold War. Remember her showing her *cojones* to the Cubans after they shot down a couple of anti-Castro planes? Aren't you tired of taking verbal abuse from rogue states? Albright will give 'em what for with militant slogans."

"How about Bill Cohen at Defense," I asked.

"Prudent man. Make a few small slices in the Defense budget, which as a Republican he can get away with easier than a Democrat can. No wars in the offing, but we'll talk about fighting two at the same time. Not to worry. After Vietnam, the Pentagon learned not to fight anyone who fights back."

"And Tony Lake as CIA chief?" I inquired. "Will he run into trouble because of not telling Congress about Iranian arms shipments to Bosnian Muslims two years ago and not selling stocks that could cause conflict of interest? Pennsylvania Republican Senator Arlen Specter who heads the Intelligence oversight committee and Alabama's Richard Shelby who will succeed him have mentioned these themes."

"No," he said. "They're fronts for Lake's real enemies. The hearings will focus on Bosnia and unsold stocks, but at CIA headquarters the boys don't want some college professor as chief spook. Also, during the Vietnam War, Lake resigned from the National Security Council, embarrassing one Henry Kissinger. Now there's a man who knows how to get revenge."

"And Bill Richardson? Is the UN a pay-back for rescuing hostages in faraway places?"

"Richardson's Hispanic, a vote that helped Clinton win big in some states. The UN gives Richardson high visibility, and a posh apartment in the Waldorf. He's carried Clinton's water and the prez rewarded him."

"And Daley, at Commerce."

"He'll bring Midwest multinationals into the trading game. These appointments have the new National Security Adviser Sandy Berger's stamp. He got Clinton through the first term with his form of pragmatic talmudism—do what you do and shrug your shoulders if it doesn't work."

"Does Clinton have an agenda?" I asked.

"Of course. Clinton wants to keep his wife out of prison, not spend all his money on lawyers, not have his private parts, I mean sex life, exposed in this Paula Jones thing. And as the Bible says, 'there is a reason Trade, Trade, Trade,' " he laughed, "so he'll have lots of good job offers from the multinational tycoons when he leaves the White House."

"A lot to look forward to," I said.

Saul Landau

Defending Clinton's Right to Rent

December 19, 1996

Why the big flap just because the First Couple rented out rooms to raise money for the presidential campaign? First, as all Americans know, winning is the only thing—especially when it comes to presidential elections. Second, the Clintons didn't just rent rooms to anyone! No one can accuse our chief exec of converting his mansion into a homeless shelter.

Indeed, an overnight stay at the president's residence cost well into the six figures. That fact alone assures us that only the finest people would place their pajama-clad bodies under the White House down.

Face it, the president and first lady were simply following the trend of the times. If you have a spare room, you rent it and use the money for your child's college tuition or, in the Clinton's case, to win the presidential election. It's not as if they sold part of the White House. They sort of leased it for an evening to people who sought the pleasure of sleeping next to power.

Yet, nagging questions persisted—like who owns the White House? If it's public property, how come the president—or the Democratic National Committee—gets the rent and not the taxpayers?

"Well, it's not exactly rent," I explained to myself. "It's a donation to the worthy cause of the president's re-election."

"Anyway," I said, "I'm sure it was just an informal arrangement between the fund raisers and the big donor." Doubts persisted.

"Maybe they actually had a system worked out," I said to myself.

So I went to the White House. A friend who works there whispered in my ear.

"It's an informal price list," he said, producing an elegant leather-bound folder.

"Wow," I said, "a ride on Air Force One with president—$500,000. Nine Holes of Golf with prez—$550,000, 18 holes—$650,000."

White House Lincoln Room for two, one night—$750,000. Includes dinner with first couple and continental breakfast in bed. Sausage and eggs breakfast with the president and first lady in White House Dining Room only $100,000 more. Morning jog with Clinton only 10K extra.

"Is this legal?" I asked. "Forget that, has any president ever done this before?"

"Well," he said, "Warren G. Harding let hookers sleep in some of the spare bedrooms in 1921."

"Yes," I said. "But Harding paid them."

"Times have changed," my friend said. "Now people pay the prez. And they take home a photo to show their grandchildren."

"Just out of curiosity," I inquired, "was there a *menage a trois* rate? Did they sell foursomes as well—for half a million more?"

"It's worth a lot of money for already rich people to get close to the president," he said.

I agreed. I now understood that White House room renting transcended re-election fundraising. It assured Clinton his place in history, alongside Harding and other great presidents like Millard Filmore and Franklin Pierce.

Saul Landau

Revolutionaries or Terrorists?

December 23, 1996

Hostage taking yields headlines. But the erosion of human life caused by starvation or curable disease—that's not hard news. Occasionally, journalists refer to Peru as an economic success story, albeit one still suffering from extreme income disparities.

Where to direct one's outrage? At the hostage-taking Tupac Amaru, or the Peruvian government and its economic system, which places the poor majority at the mercy of a market economy dominated by transnational giants?

The dramatic embassy seizure draws media, which then spins the story in yet a third way: dramatic, albeit Marxist-Leninist fanatics confronting the tough but democratic Peruvian President Alberto Fujimori.

Terrorism "experts" appear on TV and warn that "Negotiations set dangerous precedents." U.S. officials declare, "you never negotiate with terrorists." The recent Latin American past is rife with embassy or government building seizures. Sometimes negotiations take place and everyone leaves unharmed; or, governments attack, fearing that negotiating would induce future takeovers. Lots of people then die. Perhaps, the Tupac Amaru didn't watch TV on those nights and didn't learn that lesson? Or it didn't scare them.

The Tupac Amaru are prepared to die to free their *compañeros*, locked in Fujimori's notorious dungeons. Meanwhile, their hostages learn the meaning of incarceration—without proper sanitation, food, medical care.

The media informs us that Fujimori, and other presidents in Latin America, have finally brought stability to the violence-wracked continent. Occasionally, a slip occurs. Some four years ago, Fujimori seized control of the government when opposition members refused to follow his orders; or, his soldiers get caught slaughtering or torturing—and then receive rapid amnesties for their deeds. No matter. In Peru, elections occur periodically,

Parliament meets and contending political parties debate the nuances of the free market model. Oh, and the stock market has found its equilibrium. Could anyone ask more of Latin American leaders?

Experts contend that Fujimori's hard line against the Maoist Shining Path and the Fidelista Tupac Amaru has won him wide support. Experts don't talk about tens of millions living in squalor, or unemployment rates of 40%—the conditions that gave rise to guerrilla war. Not hard news.

In the global south, 35,000 people a day die of hunger. Not a headline grabber. Our civilized system does not mobilize to stop the starvation of children, but spends trillions on arms production, which it sells to poor countries to use against their own people. Not a page one story.

Some four centuries ago Tupac Amaru rebelled against the Spanish conquerors. His erstwhile descendants now hold some of the new conquerors as hostages. For whom does the church bell toll in Lima's plaza?

Saul Landau

Trade Lifts the Poor?

December 31, 1996

I step over a homeless man, insert money in the box and read the headline in the Sunday December 29 *Washington Post*. "Free Trade Helps Lift World Poor." The poor sleeping man has not yet read the paper. Otherwise, he would surely have raised his head in acknowledgment.

The illustrating photo shows a destitute woman near her hut, adjacent to a luxury, high rise hotel. "Foreign capital has reduced poverty in East Asia," the caption says, "but often bypasses the unskilled." Ah, if only the poor woman had skill!

The good news, the World Bank says, is that only 29% of the world's population are desperately poor, down 1% from 1987. The bad news is that because of population growth the number of poor in that category has drastically increased, but no more than 1.3 billion people live on less than $1 a day.

The *Post* story says that millions of skilled workers have profited from the massive investment in Philippine industry. Instead of leading sustainable but boring lives in villages, these lucky people enjoy urban shopping malls and gaze at U.S. TV programs on oversized screens inside their minute high rise apartments.

The new factory workers came from villages —once the core of Philippine society and economy. In previous decades, however, Japanese and Taiwanese fish trawlers dredged fish from Philippine waters, while factory owners dumped their waste into the same offshore area. Well, progress can be brutal. The weak shrimp and fish couldn't take the industrial goo they had to eat and live in. They died. Fishing villages became unsustainable.

But wealthy Japanese loved their prawns. So entrepreneurs designed shrimp farms, which required enormous quantities of fresh water. In turn, shrimp farming depleted water tables in coastal towns.

In the old and backward days, villagers traded fish for rice, clothes or nets. These antiquated villagers maintained large families, sustained centuries long rituals and engaged in other bonding practices that had nothing to do with shopping. Progress demanded that they move to cities where, as civilized people, they work fourteen hour days in textile mills. According to a 1993 International Labor Rights Fund report, kids as young as four fill so-called sweat shops. Needless to say, the Philippine free market hardly permits labor unions in the new industrial zones.

The *Post* article concludes that the market miracle has made the poor and the rich grow richer. Well, it's at least half true. Miraculous, I agree, that a tiny minority of global plutocrats have escaped retribution from the many.

But there is logic in the apparent madness. In 1971 Brazilian President Medici was asked why he pursued his neo-liberal plan that brought such misery to the poor. Medici explained that his plan had been very good for Brazil, but not so good for Brazilians.

The Marijuana Axiom

January 2, 1997

Picture Yale Law School in the early 1970s. After a study session, the mostly liberal-minded students draw from a large hookah pipe seated in the middle of the living room floor. Bill can't seem to get the smoke past his mouth. The others laugh at him. He laughs as well—a contact high.

In that era, the more adventurous and curious smoked pot and dropped acid. They still do, according to recent surveys.

Yale law students went on to become successful lawyers, or politicians. One former boo puffer got to the Supreme Court, although the Senate panel didn't question him extensively on how he once got high. Rather, they focused on his peculiar office behavior—especially with women.

No, I'm not reopening the Clarence Thomas issue, nor lecturing on the virtues of smoking marijuana. I'm not a states rights advocate, either, even though President Clinton has ordered the Justice Department to circumvent the California and Arizona voters' wishes to allow doctors to prescribe marijuana for certain illnesses. Where, by the way, is the conservative outcry that accompanies federal policies that interfere with local control — say on taxation?

The marijuana issue has little to do with the drug's ill or good effects on public health, conservative or liberal thinking or even the end of the Cold War.

Marijuana's illegal status, like witches in 17th Century Salem, has become an axiom of state policy: unchallengeable.

Consider the FBI and DEA, Treasury Department cops, state, county and local narcotics squads and inter agency drug task forces. Calculate the number of assistant U.S. attorneys, state, country and city prosecutors, bailiffs, judges, court reporters, prison wardens, guards and those who build prisons—all linked to current drug laws. Then, there's lab technicians, drug test administrators and educators who make anti-drug ads.

Think of the bevy of Hollywood and TV writers, actors, directors, camera operators etc. who earn their livelihood off drug dramas. Don't forget the vast criminal drug apparatus. Hundreds of thousands of Americans link their livelihood to the unquestioned fact that intake, sale or preparation of marijuana, like cocaine, crack, heroine, LSD and a variety of other substances will forever remain as criminal activity.

Vast Washington bureaucracies down to rural Mississippi drug squads have built enormous stakes in maintaining public expenditures for using drugs, beginning with arrests, trials, long and in many cases mandatory imprisonment.

Given the political power that radiates from that investment, why should we think that even as courageous a president as Clinton would allow his nostalgia for the good old days to cloud his thinking, forgive the pun, when he, Hillary, Clarence Thomas and other Yalies experienced brief reveries after closing their Torts textbook?

Face it, you youngsters out there, the 60s are dead—except for songs, posters and parents telling stories about the good old days of sex, drugs and rock and roll. You wanna change the marijuana laws: keep at it. We don't have witch trials anymore. Well, hardly any.

Saul Landau

Food Policy: Let 'Em Eat Ho-Hos

January 7, 1997

Let me read a passage from a letter from Agriculture Secretary Dan Glickman to the December 1995 worldwide food conference in Rome, held under the auspices of the UN Food and Agriculture Organization. "The United States believes that the attainment of any right to adequate food is a goal or aspiration to be realized progressively." U.S. delegates went on to promote agribusiness, not state intervention, to answer world food problems.

Cuban President Fidel Castro, on the other hand, called for resistance against the control of world food by transnational corporations under the auspices of the Word Trade Organization, the WTO. Castro insisted that food is a basic human right.

A U.S. delegate snorted. "The United States does not recognize food as a human right."

"You mean," I asked, "that a crying baby has no right to milk, a two-year-old child should not aspire to eat?"

"God provided the market to deal with food. Transnational giants dominate the market because they're stronger. Darwin, you recall. The market has improved world food allocation," he told me proudly. "In 1974, 850 million people suffered from chronic malnutrition. Now, we have only 809 million always hungry people. In twenty years, we'll cut that number in half."

"Hold it," I protested. "At the 1974 world food summit, delegates pledged to eliminate starvation in ten years. Now, with all the technological advances in food production, the best we can hope for is 400+ million near starving people?"

"The cause of the problem," he declared, "was socialist food policies."

"Huh?" I said.

"Socialist ways of thinking led to state intervention in agriculture, subsidizing of small, inefficient farmers and creating large unruly state farms. Low productivity resulted," he explained. "Socialism caged the creative giant called the market."

"In recent years, what has this magical market done?" I protested. "Massive dislocation, hunger, unemployment."

"Takes time," he assured me, "and suffering builds character in those people. Displaced peasants end up in cities, more civilized places, even for the hungry."

"When's the last time you missed a meal?" I asked.

"I skipped lunch three times last month," he said boastfully. "Notice how my spare tire has shrunk!"

"Seriously," I said. "You've ceded control over world food production and distribution not to the invisible hand of the market but to the World Trade Organization, a front for agribusiness, a handful of giant Transnational corporations. They've never shown concern for the rights of the hungry to have food.

"Imagine 2015, when 100 million more people eat packaged bread. Sales of U.S.-made dental floss will soar!"

"But," I protested, "under the U.S. plan hundreds of millions won't even get a slice of bread."

"Well," he chirped, "as some famous advertising executive once said: 'let them eat Ho-Hos.' "

Saul Landau

Is Dirty Talk Covered By Free Speech?

January 9, 1997

Like millions of porno-hating first amendment lovers, I went to see *The People v. Larry Flynt*. The film glorifies this psychotic smut peddler and simultaneously makes a passionate defense of free speech. In the movie we see a strange cross section of the public, the weirdos who surround the Flynt obscenity enterprises and live off its profits, those whose tastes or proclivities revolve around female degradation, and the militant censors.

The anti-naked crowd falls under the late H.L. Mencken's definition of Puritanism: The haunting fear that someone, somewhere might be happy. Among the leading members of this group of zealots is one Charles Keating, who went to prison for committing massive savings and loan fraud. Between the smut peddlers and the Puritans, the film makers come down on the side of smut—as free speech.

In one scene Woody Harrelson, who plays Larry Flynt, presents a slide show, intercutting photos of war victims with nudie shots. "Which," he rhetorically asks his hand-picked audience, "is the real pornography?"

Well, he didn't have to convince me. But as much as I believe that war is the ultimate obscenity, the Larry Flynt film made me feel uneasy. It offered choices like war versus porno photos as if that was our real option.

I recalled the old story about two elderly Jews seated on a subway train in New York just before the outbreak of World War II. One, reading the liberal Jewish paper, notices that the other is reading the *Brooklyn Eagle* a notorious pro-Nazi rag.

The offended man accuses the *Brooklyn Eagle* reader, "How could you read that rotten anti-Semitic filth, which praises Nazis who kill and murder Jews? That paper should be banned."

"Banned?" he asks incredulously. "Are you kidding? You read in your newspaper about the Jews being persecuted everywhere, how they're being killed, put in concentration camps. The *Brooklyn Eagle* says the Jews have taken over the world's banks, we've monopolized the arts and are about to take over the world. So, you choose to read the news that says how helpless we are, I read about how powerful we are."

I think our choices are wider. The Larry Flynt film will tell most viewers, I hope, how healthy they are and how sick the rest of the country is. Except for his civil liberties-loving lawyer, there are no normal people in the film.

Is that what America is really like? Well, maybe I travel in narrow circles.

The first amendment protects me and allows for whatever passes for civilized dialogue in this country. But the movie equates free speech with commerce. Larry Flynt published *Hustler* and his other T&A mags to make money, not to make a political statement.

Can our culture distinguish between the right to express political or artistic ideas and the right to print anything as long as there is a market for it? Well, go see the film and decide.

Saul Landau

Post-Inaugural Reflections on Defense

January 10, 1997

During World War II, the Soviet people—remember them?—mustered the will and courage to defeat the superior Nazi enemy—but what a cost.

In World War II, the Soviets lost over 20 million—out of a total population of 160 million. The Nazis destroyed 200 Soviet cities. In 1945-46, millions of Soviets lacked food and shelter. We suffered less than half a million casualties.

Nevertheless, miraculously, these cunning Reds, directed by Stalin the Butcher, mounted a military threat to western civilization, centered in Moscow. Two years earlier *My Weekly Reader* referred to Uncle Joe, who led our Soviet allies against the Nazi aggressors in a heroic defense of their homeland and western civilization.

Forty plus years of Cold War nuclear fear and trembling took a toll. Like millions of others, I practiced air raid drills, hid under my school desk, marveled at the ever newer weapons systems to make us more secure. Periodic investigations revealed Soviet infiltration, spying and subversion. Indeed, the Soviets did penetrate U.S. defense agencies and glean key military secrets— even after their demise.

Hey, they had to maintain the facade of military rivalry. I say facade because according to our government the Soviets threatened to invade and overrun Western Europe. That's why we organized NATO and sent SAC bombers with nuclear payloads to the edge of Soviet air space—round the clock.

We spent trillions defending against an enemy that collapsed without us firing a shot against their armed forces.

Once in a while, a skeptical U.S. official would note an odd fact. The Soviets never made their railroad gauges correspond to those of their East European satellites. Imagine, a Soviet invasion of Western Europe! At the East German border, for example, laborers would have to unload supplies, pile them onto trucks and then reload them again onto east European railroads.

Why didn't the Soviets equalize the width of the rail gauges? The unmatching gauges logically would also stall yet another invasion from Germany, whose troops had twice this century sent its forces deep into their territory.

Fact? Don't bother us with facts. Since the Cold War, political aspirants have accepted the premise of strong, meaning costly, defense. Who would think about economizing to save western civilization itself? But after the 1989 Soviet implosion you would have expected someone to demand to cut the military slice of our budget.

No such miracle. The Pentagon brass and their civilian adjuncts now defend their $260 billion-a-year budgets by referring to "the dangerous world out there." Adam and Eve could have said the same thing after they got tossed out of Eden. Luckily that kind of money didn't exist back then or the earth's population would have faced Chapter 11 before we reached Chapter 3 of the Bible.

Well, we don't want to confuse new generations with facts and logic gleaned from the past!

Saul Landau

The CIA Endorsed Torture?

January 28, 1997

I was shocked to read this week's *Baltimore Sun* revelations that in 1983 a CIA manual advised our Latin American military and police allies to use physical and mental torture to extract information from thousands of suspects. The U.S. military had used a similar method in the 1980s to train foreign police in executions, torture, blackmail and other methods generally frowned upon by the civilized world.

Jesus H. Ankleworm, my CIA source, raised his cadaverous frame to its 6'5" height and huffed. "We reject physical torture because it lowers the moral caliber of organizations. Besides torture's less fun than psychological game playing. In any case, those jerks shouldn't have written it down in a manual."

"Is that all you think was wrong?" I asked.

"There's a difference," he said, "between torture and psychological techniques designed to persuade the subject to want to furnish us with the information we desire. Forcing prisoners to remain standing for hours, holding them in solitary and subjecting them to extremes in heat and cold—that bothers middle-class Americans, but it's diddly squat to Latin Americans."

"You don't believe in freezing or cooking people into submission," I queried, "or making people so lonely that they'll squeal on their own mothers?"

"Not much fun in that and bad PR if it gets out" he said. "That's why the CIA revised the torture manual in 1985."

I read a line from the rewritten manual: "While we deplore the use of coercive techniques, we do want to make you aware of them so that you may avoid them."

"Did you expect officers of Honduran Battalion 316, whose members have a long record of torture and executions, to understand such details?"

"The lads got carried away. Saving the free world and all that crap," he said. "I admit, some of our boys like inflicting a drop of pain. But not the elite corps."

"What does the CIA elite want?" I asked.

"Job satisfaction," he replied. "For forty years we played Cold War with the KGB. Getting them to defect, faking defection, catching triple and quadruple agents. Exciting, all-encompassing stuff. Latin America—that's where the second team played, men who didn't get the nuances of the job."

"Their job wasn't to beat the commies everywhere?" I asked.

"Of course, the anti-commie game sustained the CIA community. But not winning guerrilla wars. The point was to keep them going, like the larger Cold War. Only naive zealots and sadists believed that the `threat to western civilization' nonsense justified torturing people to get information we already had. Like the KGB, we played chess," Ankleworm offered. "Weaken the enemy with mind games and moves."

He sighed, nostalgically. "Great sport while it lasted. Now these revelations on torture in such an insignificant part of the world. You know, no CIA or KGB official tortured each other—a gentleman's match." A tear dripped down his cheek as he walked out into the cold.

Saul Landau

Buying Democracy in Cuba

February 3, 1997

The U.S. government has announced a plan to pay up to $8 billion to Cuba. Under Title II of last year's Helms-Burton Act to help the Cuban people, Congress would authorize this money as soon as Cuba complied with minimum requirements. To qualify, the Cuban people only need to create a transition government and a market economy.

A visiting Cuban exchange scholar shared his thoughts with me on this fabulous project.

"You come home and find a 'You Won the Sweepstakes' notice," he said. "Open the envelope. The fine print requires a few steps to collect."

"What steps," I asked.

"For $8 billion," he said, "all Cubans have to do is overthrow their government."

"Does it tell you how?" I asked.

"Not exactly," he replied. "But $8 billion certainly provides incentive to dissolve the State Security apparatus and hold elections within eighteen months—and of course let U.S. observers monitor them."

"The CIA has tried in vain for decades to get rid of Castro," I said. "Do you think the Cuban people could do it?"

"Well," he said, "on $8 billion all 11 million islanders could live like kings. On the other had, we'd have to sell our public property and the only Cubans with money to buy live in Florida. We'd also have to stop jamming TV Marti, the program the U.S. Information Agency beams to us that we've never seen."

"What's so bad about that?" I asked.

"Some suspect that it's a porn channel and only the Politburo gets to see it. Funny," he said, "the U.S. government wants us to see TV Marti to understand democracy, but doesn't let live Americans, who could tell us the same things, travel to Cuba."

He continued. "Helms-Burton has a hidden agenda. We have one political party. Imagine all the Communist Party factions became parties, say 50. Add 500 parties for the Miami exiles. We'd have almost as many parties as Imelda Marcos had shoes. *Qué fiesta más grande*! What an election that would be!"

"To pass qualifying tests we'd establish PACs and lobbies, the essence of your democracy. The U.S. would have to allow large corporations to come to Cuba with money to start these influence peddling groups."

"I don't get it," I said. "Explain."

"Well, Cuban doctors have no equivalent of the AMA; there's no real estate or bankers' lobby, or defense lobbies to ensure that we establish missile systems. We don't even have a national rifle association or an anti-abortion lobby. You see how far we have to go to qualify?"

"Hmm," I said.

"What's more," he said, "candidates aspiring to office would need millions to pay for mud-slinging campaigns on TV."

"Wow," I said, "Cuba has a lot of work to do before qualifying."

"And, even if we complied," he said, "what guarantees that Congress would vote the money? Remember, Bush promised payoffs to Nicaragua and eastern Europe if they changed governments. Kissinger promised Vietnam billions in reparations. They got *casi nada*."

"That's Spanish," I said. "What does it mean in English?"

"Bupkis, buddy, that's what this is all about."

Saul Landau

Life, aka Soap

February 6, 1997

After the president delivered his State of the Union address, my friend called, sounding desperate: "I can't believe it's over."

"You mean Clinton's speech," I replied.

"No, silly," he responded, "the OJ trials. With OJ's drama done, I have no continuity in life. How will I make it through the week?"

"Read the comics," I offered, "Follow pro basketball box scores or pick a stock and follow its ups and downs in the business section. How about concentrating on your work?"

"That was easy when I worked for IBM. Then they downsized. It was OK at AT&T, designing phone computers, until they laid off forty thousand. 'Nothing personal,' the guy who gave me the pink slip said."

"Now one day I program octane ratings for an oil company; the next day I prepare figures so insurance executives can decide if they should buy London real estate or Jamaican bauxite. This week I'm bagging groceries at Safeway."

"How about your family?" I asked.

"That fell apart when IBM laid me off."

"What's this got to do with the OJ verdict?" I asked.

"The OJ case had everything I don't have in my life," he said. "Hot sex, lurid drugs, family violence."

"You mean," I said, "you saw the OJ trials as symbols?"

"Damned right," he said. "My life doesn't measure up to OJ's—or Nicole's for that matter."

"You mean you lack excitement, glamour, wealth in your daily routine? You need to murder your ex wife, get framed by the police and face a couple of trials that hundreds of millions of people watch to feel satisfied? You want to be a victim," I said, "a black man so Dirty Harry can routinely bust you? That's sick."

"I am a victim," he said, "but without the spotlight. I've even thought of appearing on an afternoon TV talk show to reveal my darkest secrets—just to be someone. I used to feel satisfied with my life as an engineer with a regular job.

"Downsizing affected my self image. Following OJ and all the lawyers on TV, reading their own dramatic stories—kind of revived me."

"You mean, you crave a vicarious existence."

"Yes," he said. "It's better than no existence. Reality for me doesn't coincide with Bill Clinton's picture. Yes, our dynamic economy has created millions of new jobs, but mostly temporary ones without health plans and pensions. Nothing endures," he whined. "I had hoped the OJ story would last forever."

"It's not over yet," I said. "Rumor has OJ planning to run for Congress—to earn quick money to pay off the civil trial damages."

"Oh, good," he said, "More drama ahead. Like Clinton said, there's still hope."

Saul Landau

Money Doesn't Talk, It Screams

February 13, 1997

With the Cold War over, we've switched our all-encompassing national value from anti-communism to love of money.

Take my yuppie friend who hated New York because people there talk only about money and their psychiatrists. In Los Angeles, she said, people don't discuss their psychiatrists. As the late Sam Goldwyn said: Anyone who goes to a psychiatrist ought to have his head examined.

In LA, Buddhist monks buy political influence with presidential candidates, as if money opens the road to Nirvana.

When the OJ Simpson jury decided on $25 million against the former sports hero, character actor and #1 Hertz salesman, money made headlines because, in the immortal Vince Lombardi's words, it's not everything, it's the only thing. Imagine 200 million people all trying to visualize $25 million.

How would our consumer society function if it weren't consumed by money? If we couldn't shop 24 hours a day, at all-night Kmarts or through the shopping channels, what would keep people from going crazy with anxiety? What would hold families together? What would they do on Saturday and after church on Sunday? When God said honor the Sabbath, He meant shop on Sundays, unless you're Jewish or Adventist—in which case shop on Saturday.

Shopping is also patriotic. If we didn't wisely spend our incomes on clothing, appliances, jewelry, fast foods, casinos, cars, RVs, motor boats and software, we could lose our number one status.

Indeed, we know what to do with money.

New York Yankee manager Casey Stengel asked his catcher Yogi Berra: What would you do if you found a million dollars?

I'd find the fellow who lost it, Berra replied, and if he was poor, I'd return it.

Look at sports. For thousands of years humans competed to show strength, will, skill, coordination and courage. Now sports has evolved into a business. "I'll fight him for nothing if the price is right." WBA welterweight Marlon Starling commented on his upcoming title fight. Dennis Rodman paid $200,000 to the photographer he kicked in the groin. "He could kick me there twice for that money," a friend of mine said. Poor Dennis lost his endorsement contracts—millions of dollars gone with one little kick.

Money, the root of all evil, the stuff that makes the world go round, rewards and punishments, a pound of flesh. Jesus wanted to get money changers out of the temple, but not money itself. Churches suck up fortunes from their flocks. Money buys presidents. People marry, divorce and, of course, kill for it.

Money became the ultimate denouement in the OJ Simpson drama—the longest running soap opera in recent history. And, as OJ himself said, it's not over yet.

What will the next soap be about—sex, violence, politics, or all three?

Saul Landau

Campaign Finance; What Future?

February 18, 1997

"Mention campaign finance reform and the image emerges of the $2 plus billion donated by corporations and banks to last year's campaigns. Is this why government gives to the rich and not the poor, who cannot afford to make mammoth contributions?" I asked my guru, Dr. Izzy Knowitall.

"You sound naive, or worse, un-American," he said. "Imagine a tobacco chief executive who can't buy political influence! Explain that to the stockholders and Jerry Falwell."

"But in the 1990s," I countered, "PACs and lobbying shouldn't exclude the majority from meaningful participation."

"Please," he said. "The Founding Fathers were terrified that the rabble would rule and take away their ill-gotten wealth. Propertyless people couldn't vote until the 1820s, women until the 1920s and blacks not until the late 1960s."

"Come on," I said. "You believe that a snot-nosed kid who inherits millions of shares of tobacco stock has the right to bribe, I mean contribute, half a million simoleons to Jesse Helms, who will claim that the anti-tobacco campaign is a communist and homosexual plot? Next thing, the tobacco lobby will find doctors who'll say cancer is good for you."

"What's freedom about," said Dr. Knowitall, "if not freedom to buy a member of Congress or even the president himself?"

"How about Chinese businessmen," I said, "who invest in Arkansas natural gas and buy the attorney general and continue influencing him even when he's in the White House?"

"Hey," said Izzy, "foreigners don't have the right to buy Congress and the president. What do you take me for, a one-worlder? But campaign finance reform is a joke."

"Wait," I said. "We proclaim our democracy as the greatest in world history, but our reality has a bunch of rich special interests using that system to get even richer."

"I remember President Warren G. Harding—God rest his soul," he said nostalgically. "Harding played poker with business tycoons who lost money to him every week. He'd let them sleep off their drunks in White House bedrooms. He even kept fancy ladies around for them. That was before these post-modern PACs and manipulation by hocus focus groups."

"What does Bill Clinton have to lose by going for real campaign finance reform?"

"He could lose the guarantee of his pardon, that's what. Clinton doesn't need campaign money, but Gore does and it's Gore who'll have to pardon this Arkansas gonif."

"So, you don't think Clinton or Congress will make campaign finance reform their number one priority?"

"Sure kid, and by December we'll have won the drug war, put Washington on a sound financial basis, forged a lasting Middle East peace, and achieved racial harmony. By the way," he says, "the pharmaceutical industry is throwing a bash for Al Gore tonight, Wanna go?"

"Maybe so," I said. "Will there be some good drugs there? After what you said, I think I need some."

Saul Landau

Michael Manley—R.I.P.

March 10, 1997

He succumbed to prostate cancer, the ugly fiend that grows in the mysterious areas where men's bodily functions become anatomically bewildered. But Michael Manley's mind never lost its lucid quality.

Mainstream media obituaries say that the once-proud advocate of third world nationalism and democratic socialism became a free market convert, referring to the period from 1989-1992 when he was reelected as prime minister of Jamaica and accepted the IMF-World Bank formula for running the economy.

I always doubted his public pronouncements about courting foreign capital and distancing himself from his friend Fidel Castro. In a 1989 interview with Bob Borosage and me, he half-heartedly espoused the neo liberal model. Then, in frustration, he said: "Our budget limitations present us with the painful choice between rebuilding the roads destroyed by last year's hurricane or raising the teachers' salaries and thus keeping them in school. We lack the resources to do both." Off the record, Manley confessed that just to get the $29 million in aid for the war on drugs "we must cooperate with the Drug Enforcement Agency."

Cancer forced Manley to resign, which I think he did with relief. He renewed his friendship with Fidel, tried to help Haitian President Aristide return to his rightful place and again became a voice for the poor of the global South.

In 1976 and 1980 I made Michael Manley's campaign films. I traveled throughout Jamaica, filming him in Accompang, a village high in the central mountains; speaking with Maroons, descendants of escaped slaves from the 19th century. At night he delivered stem-winders in the slums of Kingston, where the air filled with ganja smoke, insuring that everyone got at least a contact high.

Manley presented "democratic socialism," a program that included housing and medical support for the poor, and a plan to induce slum dwellers back to the land on subsistence size plots.

Michael Manley explained to Jamaicans why they had to support Cuba (because Cuba helped third world independence movements), why Jamaica had to be energetic in its role in the non-aligned movement and back the ANC in South Africa and the independence movement of Zimbabwe.

Manley told me that he detected the first CIA destabilization campaign against his government in 1976 as the result of his support for Fidel Castro's sending of Cuban troops to Angola.

According to Fidel Castro, Angolan President Agostinho Neto called him, asking for Cuba's aid to stop the South African and Zairean invasion into the newly-independent former Portuguese colony. After the Central Committee approved, Castro phoned Manley and asked him to back the daring move. Manley agreed.

Cuban troops stopped the South African and Zairean forces, both aided by the CIA, and thus helped the new Angolan government to consolidate power.

Henry Kissinger flew into a rage. In December 1975, he was vacationing at the Rockefeller estate in Jamaica and met with Manley, pleading for Jamaican support for a U.S.-sponsored UN Security Council resolution condemning the Cuban action. Since Jamaica was a Security Council member at the time, Manley's support was crucial. Manley turned him down and maintained his support for Castro's position in Angola.

Kissinger and the CIA neither forgot nor forgave. In 1980, Manley cited CIA-backed violence, U.S. economic pressure and a psychological warfare campaign as having bred fear and hatred in Jamaica and turned the Jamaican electorate against him. He lost the election.

I filmed and recorded some of the results of the campaign— hundreds of corpses and a society trembling with fear.

I remember Manley for being the foremost advocate for socialism in the English-speaking world during the 1970s and 1980s, for moving the British commonwealth against apartheid in South Africa and for his being a loving and passionate man in the cause of economic and racial justice.

The obituary in the *Washington Post* remembers him for changing his position at the end of his life, a distortion which deprives us and our young of Manley and Jamaica's real history.

Michael Manley wrote a book about the costs of bucking U.S. power called *Jamaica: Struggle in the Periphery*. Read it and learn lessons about imperialism and the costs of fighting against it.

Michael Manley died on March 6, 1997. They called him Joshua, a reference to the Biblical hero whose trumpet brought down the walls of Jericho. Michael Manley's trumpet was his voice, which reflected his mind. "Glory to socialism," he used to say at the end of his speeches.

The FMLN Wins Elections

March 17, 1997

The Farabundo Marti Front for National Liberation appears to have won yesterday's national and municipal elections in El Salvador. Early vote counts indicate that the former revolutionaries turned electoral moderates just squeaked past the right-wing Arena Party. President Armando Calderon Sol congratulated the FMLN on their victory.

Shafik Handal, once a guerrilla commander, declared that electoral results constituted "an important message for the democratization process of our country."

The newly elected radical mayor of San Salvador declared that "we are going to build a different city, one which we'll be proud of."

Only seven years ago some of the suit and tie wearing candidates wore uniforms and carried AK 47s. They belonged to a revolutionary movement, backed by Soviet supplies and animated by the example of Cuba. They denounced U.S. imperialism and put forth socialist programs, based on the ideas of their messiah Farabundo Marti—who was a Communist.

These same people today visit Washington and chat with State Department officials, visit the IMF and World Bank offices. Yes, the world has undergone a drastic change in less than a decade.

Socialism is not just absent from FMLN campaign rhetoric, but has disappeared as a political option for them as well. Like the electoral left of most other Latin American countries, the FMLN has accepted the neo-liberal world as it is and will formulate policies accordingly.

FMLN partisans sing victory songs: "*El pueblo unido jamás será vencido.*" "The people united shall never be defeated." But at what a cost—and how much unity exists among the people today after a narrowly won election? One thinks of the nearly 100,000 who died in the decade-long civil war. As their corpses now decompose in El Salvador's soil, will their memory serve to keep the living from falling prey to the corruption that has engulfed so many other newly-emerging democracies?

Some of the ultra-leftists who, in 1975, accused the poet Roque Dalton of working for the CIA, and then executed him, have emerged as legislators and mayors.

Before he died, Roque Dalton wrote a poem called TODOS, All of us. It's worth recalling on the day of celebration and worth repeating every day because it might help to keep the FMLN officials focused as they receive the temptations that follow office.

> Let us unite the half dead who are this country
> That we may be worthy of calling ourselves your children
> In the name of the murdered
> Let us unite against all the murderers of all
> All of us together
> Have more death than they
> But all of us together
> Have more life than they

The Farabundo Marti Front for National Liberation will have its chance to put these words, written by Roque Dalton, over two decades ago, into action—for life, not death in El Salvador.

Double Standards on Elections

March 24, 1997

Does God punish bad guys? How about FBI agents investigating Indiana Republican Dan Burton, God-fearing, co-author of the Helms-Burton Law, on charges of shaking down Pakistanis for campaign contributions—and on the eve of Burton-chaired hearings on dirty foreign money for campaigns!

"How about Burton's Senate cohort Senator Jesse Helms getting tobacco money?" I asked my friend on the Federal Elections Commission.

"That's benign American money," he said. "which is different from harmful foreign money."

"How about our money going abroad to influence elections?" I asked.

"Even Jesse Helms never doubted that U.S. money should influence elections abroad," he said. "You recall, Helms objected only that it went to the wrong people. In the mid 1980s, the CIA secretly donated $2 million to Salvadoran President Jose Napoleon Duarte's campaign. Helms said Duarte was a pinko. He wanted our taxpayers' money to support the psychopathic Roberto D'Aubisson who he said better represented U.S. values."

"Well," I said, "my colleague, Norman Solomon, says that Americans see foreign money meddling in our elections as a bigger sin than say renting the Lincoln bedroom. Why don't we apply that rule to our influencing foreign elections?"

"What do the Russians know about democracy," he retorted. "If not for our millions in Yeltsin's 1996 presidential campaign, he might've lost. That would've been catastrophic."

"For the Russian people?"

"No, silly, for us. We revived that corpse and sent him our spinmeisters to create an image of a statesman. You notice the media flaks don't refer to him as a drunken former Moscow Communist Party Boss any more. Our National Endowment for Democracy uses its $30 million a year budget to assist our friends overseas. Forty-one members now sitting in the Russian parliament, for instance, received campaign aid from one of the endowment's conduits," he boasted.

"We pay Yeltsin's campaign expenses. We want to expand NATO a drop. Some Russians behave as if the Cold War still existes. Not Yeltsin. At the Summit, he took a weak stand on NATO expansion, along with the Parliamentarians we bought, I mean helped. U.S. money fosters U.S. interests abroad, I mean democracy—which eventually will take root in those barbaric places."

"According to Andrew Mollison of *Cox News Service*," I said, "we've influenced elections in more than 100 countries, including Chile, Italy, Nicaragua and Australia.

"Yes, our government gives private institutions taxpayers' money to bring in services and expert advice on strategy and polling to pro-U.S. political parties from from A to Z. We've bought elections from Albania to Zambia. "

"So, why do we get upset when Chinese or Indonesian tycoons try to do the same thing here?" I asked.

"The United States holds the copyright on election buying," he said. "Foreigners stealing our methods—that would violate intellectual property rights."

Intuition versus Trust

April 1, 1997

Freedom, I've discovered, includes freedom to live in fear. The security age means metal detectors, identification cards, heavily armed guards, barricades around the White House. I walk around terrified. Kidnappers, car jackers, muggers, child molesters, rapists and nuts who bomb federal buildings or kill their former colleagues. On top of that, I must worry about what I eat, wear, or put in my house—to say nothing of fear of global warming, vanishing whales, owls, or ozone.

Fear's a good instinct, but scientific evidence has confused us. Whom shall you believe? One day Expert A warns that eating red meat will give you cancer, heart attacks and acute indigestion. Two weeks later, Scientist B states that eating pork gives pregnant mothers food nutrition. Was Scientist A paid by the Tofu industry and B by the pork lobby?

Think of the decades-long tobacco debate. The smoker who awakened with a hacking, oyster-producing cough told his ten-year-old that scientific evidence shows links between smoking and respiratory disorders.

Tobacco companies hired stables of experts willing to declare that tobacco was good for you—along with asbestos, lead and mercury.

Those who claimed to suffer from severe symptoms after exposure to Agent Orange, the foliage-destroying chemical, had problems with their heads, said batteries of army scientists. That's actually correct. Agent Orange effects the pituitary gland, located near the brain.

In any case, who can you trust these days?

Ford marketed the Pinto with the exploding gas tank knowingly. Lisa Finaldi of *Third World Network Features* warns that Kmart sells discounted vinyl blinds that cause lead poisoning in kids.

Saul Landau

Jay Gould's book, *The Enemy Within*, refutes government experts and asserts that women living near nuclear reactors have increased incidence of breast cancer.

Millions of Americans drink bottled water because they disbelieve experts who claim their local water supply is safe. But can you trust the bottlers?

Millions more eat only organic, fearing the effects of pesticide sprays and chemical fertilizer that currently drown commercial crops. But can you place confidence in the organic producers?

Fear of old products leads to new consumption patterns, a boon for the global market, an impetus for new investment.

So, whom can you trust? Scientist A claims chocolate causes allergies. Expert B claims it'll prolong your life. Artificial whipped cream, juicy steaks from hormone-fed cows, freshly sprayed red strawberries.

You getting hungry?

What can you safely eat or wear? My advice is trust the supreme expert: yourself. Intuition in the age of ever conflicting scientific evidence is the last refuge for the citizen—if you're still free enough of science and technology to have any intuition left! Remember, Aristotle said, "Intuition is the source of scientific knowledge."

Middle East Morass

April 9, 1997

My Middle East commentaries often beget reprimands from listeners. I'm an Arab baiter, or worse, a self-hating Jew—because of something critical I've said about Israeli government policies.

So, not taking any chances, I asked Jack E. Mason, my pro-Israel-no-matter-what friend why Israeli Prime Minister Netanyahu ordered bulldozers to start new Israeli housing projects in East Jerusalem, in the midst of Palestinian territory.

"Are you kidding?" he replied. "Israel has a housing shortage. What's more important, using every spare moment of the day to make concessions to the ungrateful Palestinians just to make those ridiculous Oslo Accords work, or fulfilling sacred campaign obligations to build new Jewish housing projects? Bibi's a politician who must face the indignation of Jewish people living in crowded apartments. And what a coincidence. The only vacant land he found was in the Palestinian part of Jerusalem."

"Just a coincidence?" I asked.

"Of course," he replied. "If not for that trouble-making Arafat, may his violence-loving soul rot in hell, the Palestinians would have simply gone about their business instead of resorting to wanton acts of terrorism against innocent Jewish people."

"The rest of the world is not buying this line."

"Oh yeah? The courageous President Clinton could have put pressure on Netanyahu, but instead he blamed both sides equally, which means no one is to blame. Read Charles Krauthammer in the *Washington Post* and A. M. Rosenthal in the *New York Times*. They conclude that Arafat deserves the blame for not keeping that ignorant, no-good gang of Hamas terrorists where they belong, locked up or dead in their coffins—and who could trust a guy with a permanent five day growth anyway."

"Do you think the media covers the story accurately?" I asked.

"Sure! Listen to the Israeli flaks, I mean experts, on NPR, who offer balanced reporting that says Palestinian terrorism is terrible and it's a shame that the Oslo accords aren't working."

"But," I said, "Arab nations threaten to stop trading with Israel because of the new settlements. Europeans condemn the Netanyahu policies. Doesn't that upset you?"

"Listen. Even a principled man like Bill Clinton won't pressure Bibi because he'd face the wrath of the so-called Israeli lobby. And if the United States won't stop us, who will? So, Israel builds new housing on Palestinian land, Palestinian kids throw rocks, Israeli soldiers shoot them dead. A Hamas bomber blows himself up along with some Israeli civilians. What's new? Ecclesiastes said: 'A time to love, and a time to hate; a time of war and a time of peace.' Now is hating time and war time."

"Well," I concluded, "that's hard to dispute. Don't you worry that unless Israel takes Palestinian feelings into account, there'll be perpetual war?"

"Feelings, shmeelings! You're expecting maybe peace in your lifetime?"

Bays of Pigs to Just Piggery

April 17, 1997

Last week an indignant President Clinton explained to the press that he had imposed harsh policies on Cuba—but not on China, Vietnam or North Korea because those three countries had not murdered any Americans lately. Clinton was referring to last year's shooting down of two civilian planes flown by Cuban Americans over or near Cuban air space.

"Cuba dictates U.S. policy," Clinton said and "until I see some willingness to change, it's going to be very difficult to persuade me to change our policy. I would have a different attitude toward China, Vietnam or North Korea if they murdered any Americans."

"Wow!" I said to myself. "Clinton uses murder as policy criteria."

What a moral man. But what's his starting point?

Thirty six years ago, President Kennedy authorized the CIA to launch some 1500 Cuban exiles to land at the Bay of Pigs on Cuba's south coast. The purpose: destroy the Castro government. In the three days of fighting, Castro's forces defeated the invading army. Hundreds died.

After the Bay of Pigs fiasco, the Kennedy brothers sought revenge for their humiliation in Cuba. Under Bobby Kennedy's direction, the CIA mobilized assassins and saboteurs for missions against Castro and Cuba. President Jack and Attorney General Bob authorized thousands of operations that were the equivalent of the Oklahoma bombing—against Cuba.

"The president and his brother were ready to avenge their personal embarrassment by overthrowing the enemy at any cost," wrote Richard Bissell, CIA director of anti-Castro terrorism, in his memoirs, *Reflections of a Cold Warrior*, released by Yale University.

Bissell, a Yale graduate like the Clintons, ran Operation Mongoose, as the spooks labeled their naughtiness, referring to the agile animal that kills poisonous snakes.

According to Bissell, the Kennedys wanted to send "more saboteurs, more trained guerrillas." And, most important, Bobby demanded "results."

Bissell insists that the Kennedys personally OK'd all Mongoose actions. And Eisenhower, he informs us, was equally eager "to move against Castro."

No U.S. official went to trial for the Bay of Pigs, or for the thousands of terrorist acts that the highest officials ordered afterward. Acts done in the name of national security fall outside the realm of accountability.

So do Cuban victims of U.S. assassination and sabotage fall under Clinton's idea of murder? Will Clinton apologize for these past deeds? Don't hold your breath. After all, Cuba can't very well impose an embargo on the United States.

Cubans remember the Bay of Pigs as a great military victory over U.S.-backed invaders. As President Clinton enforces the ever more draconian embargo, think of the meaning of depriving Cuban kids of medicine. It's not exactly murder. Well, let's just it call it piggery without the Bay.

What to Do with the FBI

April 21, 1997

Fred Whitehurst, a truth-seeking laboratory professional, has shown that FBI lab technicians contaminated or even fabricated evidence in the World Trade Center and Oklahoma bombing cases and many others.

The Inspector General confirms his charges and adds that the Bureau has done additional sloppy work trying to catch spies.

Shocking! In the 1940s I listened to *The FBI in Peace and War*. On the radio G men saved us from terrible threats.

In those day, the FBI symbolized the incorruptible, persistent men (no women agents back then) who hunted Nazis and mafiosos.

I later learned that Bureau Chief J. Edgar Hoover concentrated his agents' energies on harassing the left instead of chasing crime bosses. FBI Special Agent Robert Scherrer told me that during the 1960s he would monitor elderly Jewish grandmothers in the Bronx, because they belonged to the Party.

"I felt ridiculous when one would invite me for tea and cookies and ask about my family," he admitted.

In the 1960s Hoover ordered COINTELPRO, an illegal FBI surveillance and agent provocateur operation focused on civil rights and anti-war movement leaders as well as on older leftists.

Between 1968 and 1973, the FBI planted 72 informants in the Institute for Policy Studies, where I worked. Then, in 1976, FBI agents began investigating the murders of my colleagues Orlando Letelier and Ronni Moffitt. So, when FBI Special Agent L. Carter Cornick told me he planned to interrogate Isabel Letelier, Orlando's widow, I assumed he meant to use the murders as a pretext to go after IPS or Chilean leftists in exile. He looked into my eyes.

"I don't care what happened between the Bureau and IPS," he told me. "I'm a criminal investigator. I'm going to solve this case." Against all logic, I believed him.

Under Cornick's direction, the FBI did solve the case. Indeed, two former Chilean Generals are currently in prison and a Spanish judge is hearing charges against Pinochet himself, thanks in large part to the FBI's good work in that unique and honest investigation—which occurred twenty years ago.

In the 1980s the FBI returned to its harassment of the left, especially around Central America issues.

In the 1990s, we witness how institutional rot has infected this previously sacrosanct police apparatus. But careful review of FBI history shows that it never deserved its good reputation, Cornick notwithstanding. Indeed, J. Edgar Hoover had designed a national police force whose methods were and are incompatible with democracy. Perhaps the way to reform it lies in democratizing the State, to insure that the police account directly to the public—or else, get rid of them!

Welcome to the New World Order

April 28, 1997

Did you not take seriously the order part? Well, Peruvian President Fujimori demonstrated how to correct the mistakes made by repressive U.S. forces in Waco.

Civilization will not tolerate forms of disobedience that angry and frustrated radicals have traditionally used to dramatize the diseased nature of their politics and the systematic brutality the poor endure in everyday life.

Back in the 1970s, the Sandinistas took the Nicaraguan Presidential Palace—with hostages. Much of the world applauded. A proper way to deal with a Somoza dictatorship!

In that old world order, non-democracies abounded and rated U.S. support, because dictators mouthed anti-communist rhetoric and voted with Washington in the UN.

With the New World Order that President Bush inaugurated with the technological massacre in Iraq, I mean the Gulf War, the United States symbolically announced its reduced level of tolerance for rogue states and rogue activity—everywhere.

U.S. law enforcement agencies showed they would brook no resistance at Waco and Ruby Ridge, no matter the nasty publicity that accrued from killing women and children.

The government subsequently discovered other consequences from Waco and Ruby Ridge. Avengers bombed the Oklahoma City Federal Building.

Then came the Tupac Amaru's seizure of the Japanese Ambassador's residence in Lima. It gave the New World Order's promoters an opportunity to show both their will and their technology and that they could correct tactical errors made in Waco.

The months-long drama in Peru became an ideal lesson-teacher—about new rules, about the price oppositionists will pay for serious disobedience.

Note how Peruvian President Fujimori gloated while the Peruvian soldiers celebrated over the dismembered bodies of the Tupac rebels. In case anyone wondered about what lessons

Fujimori was teaching, the beheaded corpses of the young rebels should have satisfied their curiosity. U.S. spokespeople could hardly contain their glee over the success of the Lima operation.

Reporters claim U.S. and Israeli experts on modern civilizing techniques trained the Peruvian hit squad and helped them prepare the battle plan. No one has denied the report.

I disagree with hostage-taking tactics, but I sympathized with the Tupac's desperation as revolutionaries who saw no political entry points—despite fatuous declarations that Peru is a functioning democracy.

Picture democracy in the global south: hundreds of millions of people living in squalor, unemployment rates over 40%, 35,000 people a day dying of hunger! But they can vote and occasionally there is no electoral fraud. No wonder committed people become desperate!

Some four centuries ago, Tupac Amaru rebelled against the Spanish conquerors. Rebellion in Peru has continued since then and will not end with the army's success at the Japanese Embassy. The church bell will toll for years in Lima's plaza. I think of Emily Dickinson in my salute to those brave men and women. "They perished in the seamless grass,— no eye could find the place, But God on his repealless list, Can summon every face."

The Bidness of America Is Bidness

April 29, 1997

We live in a bidness culture. See the elite at airports, where they fly bidness class, do bidness before the flight in the bidness lounge, and enjoy bidness services airlines provide to bidness travelers.

Fax, email, instant access to stock and bond trading details and free drinks to mask the tension created by today's demanding bidness culture. What oxymoron?

The bidness traveler. He leaves the limo at the airport curb while talking on cell phone—or shouting orders like buy short, sell long, carries a laptop, garment bag and small overnight case,

Mr. or Ms. Bidness strides through security, briefly turning off the cell phone, but redialing en route to the first class lounge, where a smiling young woman greets the bidness customer with obsequious effusiveness after perusing the corporate membership card.

"Not to worry," she says. "We'll notify you in time to board your flight. Are you familiar with all the bidness features of our first class lounge?"

Bloody Mary sharing table with lap top, the executive plugs into email and gets the latest sales info, stock option possibilities and gossip about the bidness people who will attend the meeting in Nashville. Other execs hold meetings in the lounge's bidness conference room.

Sip another BM, while studying the *Wall Street Journal* and using the lounge phone to retrieve messages from office voice mail. The bidness traveler makes a last check with secretary via cell phone.

Before take-off, passengers must turn off their electronic devices. The bidness traveler closes lap top, begins reviewing report on the new stock offering that will dominate the bidness meeting later in the day.

The third Bloody Mary begins to work, slowing the anxieties. Some sharp neophyte will catch the error on the profit calculation sheet or see the discrepancy between last year's sales figures and this year's projected total.

The plane begins to taxi, the smiling flight attendant collects the empty Bloody Mary glass. The bidness traveler scans the airline magazine's features for bidness travelers. Seminars on how to improve your level of self confidence, rid yourself of guilt over dishonesty before entering important meetings, make better presentations, use audio visual aids in making bidness pitches; or tapes to teach you the proper posture, dress, enunciation. Other features offer tips on how to avoid sexual harassment charges in the office and still take advantage of your superior position to extract favors from underlings.

The flight attendant announces special offers for bidness customers and thanks the passengers for giving her airline their bidness. Our bidness traveler finishes Bloody Mary number 5.

Yes, bidness feels good, sounds good. History has reached its acme. There's never been a more spiritual culture. God bless the bidness people.

CIA and Drugs Again

May 2, 1997

Last year, *San Jose Mercury News* reporter Gary Webb linked the CIA with narcotrafficking in its 1980s Contra War against Nicaragua. Webb implied that Agency personnel had encouraged crack sales in the Los Angeles ghetto. Since then, our most prestigious press and the CIA itself have attacked the accuracy of Webb's reporting. The *San Jose Mercury* semi-retracted the story.

My CIA source audio scanned the parking lot where we met.

"Was Webb right?" I asked.

"No," he said. "Webb missed the point."

"You mean," I said, "the CIA didn't encourage drug traffic to get money to supply the Contras?"

"Encourage?" He harrumphed. "When CIA personnel permitted narcotraffickers to operate in the name of getting money for the beloved Contras, they acted in the American tradition of covert operations."

"You mean drug dealing as a means to fight communism?"

"Not exactly," he said. "In the 1950s CIA scientists dosed, I mean carried out experiments with drugs on guinea pigs, I mean unsuspecting people. Some of the subjects tried unsuccessfully to fly from several stories up. In the early 1960s CIA guys in the Miami station ran drugs. During the Vietnam War, the CIA's Air American ran heroin out of the Golden Triangle. In the 1980s, CIA people ran great stuff, I mean despicable opium and hash from Afghanistan."

"You mean CIA operatives have always used drug trafficking to win the war against communism?"

"Son, you miss the point. We're a nation of entrepreneurs. Give an American cash that he doesn't have to account for, an airplane with cargo that doesn't have to clear customs and you've created a businessman—one who can transport drugs, arms, or Cuban cigars. But drugs are more profitable."

"Hold on, you mean Gary Webb got the story right?"

"Well, he overachieved. A good editor would have helped him. Basically, he had it right—except for the motive. Smart people profited from the Contra war. Doing well by doing good and all that."

"So, why did the *New York Times*, *Washington Post* and *Los Angeles Times* attack the story so vociferously?" I asked.

"Are you that innocent, son?" he said. "The establishment attacked him because even though he exaggerated on some of his claims he got too close to the real story."

"But why would the *Los Angeles Times* assign 16 reporters to attack a young journalist instead of putting them on the story itself?"

"Hey," he said, "Webb raised issues about our system, the deliberate exposure of our minorities to drugs, the decision that the Contra war took priority over the drug war. In fact, the drug war may be the quintessential covert operation. Reporting that kind of stuff is a no no. If you push links between drugs and the CIA, you might link drugs and big banks and…well gotta go."

"Maybe this attack on Webb created a cloud of smoke over the real story," I said to my pal's exhaust fumes.

The Lost Bomber

May 2, 1997

Did you share my sense of relief when the air force announced it had found the wreckage of the missing A-10 Warthog bomber somewhere in the Rocky Mountains?

I asked my Joint Chiefs of Staff contact why the air force flew missions carrying live 500-pound bombs over the United States.

"Classified," he said.

"Hey, the cold war is over," I replied.

"Well, the squadron was either en route to the practice range or else moving bombs to another location. The armed forces doesn't risk using trucks on today's highways, given the current state of carjackings and truckjackings."

"Why not practice with duds?" I asked. "After all, we have no immediate enemies."

"The air force's mission is to produce trained killers who will not hesitate to drop bombs on people. Can you imagine the humiliation our country would have suffered if our pilots had refused to drop live bombs on the Iraqis, for example? You don't get to be number one by practicing with duds."

"OK," I said. "But explain why the government authorized 400 sorties to find the guy's remains? The newspapers say you used seismic sensors, radar imaging and other sophisticated devices to locate the wreckage. That must have cost $30–40 million."

"More," he said. "But we didn't care about the pilot, only the bombs and the plane."

"Were you worried the Russians would find the plane and copy it and steal the bombs?"

"Those guys can barely wipe their own backsides these days."

"The Chinese?"

"Thirty years down the road we might worry about them," he quipped.

"Then why expend so much manpower and money," I asked.

"You ever heard of the Republic of Colorado's Patriotic Militia?"

I shook my head. "Negative."

"Well, it's classified, but apparently a group of former air force officers who saw no reason to keep paying taxes to a corrupt government has begun a conspiracy to steal some planes and carry out bombing raids on federal buildings—just to show that they care, you understand."

"Oh sure," I said.

"You see, McVeigh and Nichols and the Oklahoma Federal Building conspiracy might be just the tip of a large iceberg of ex-military people who want to show that they can make their resentment real. You gotta appreciate the patriotism, the principle, but after all..." He sighed.

"Are you saying that the major military threat to the United States is at home, our own people?"

"Well," he replied, "who else is as well armed as the American public? Who else hates the U.S. government as much as our own public?"

Remember, the great philosopher Pogo once said, "We have seen the enemy and they is us."

Immigrants: A Painful Story

May 9, 1997

"Life's not fair," says the bus poster. You see a gorgeous white teenage girl about to pout. "Learn to live with it."

Well, why should Central American immigrants fare better than our own middle class teenagers? Of course, President Clinton hasn't yet drawn up plans to deport badly behaved adolescent citizens, but the INS will soon send packing some 300,000 Central Americans.

That's what the president told his hosts recently in Central America. "Don't worry," he promised. "We'll respect their human rights, up to a point."

"But," Central American presidents protested, "our people fled U.S.-backed wars in Nicaragua, El Salvador, Guatemala. The United States turned Honduras into a U.S. base to fight those wars. Lots of our people became refugees, and Presidents Reagan and Bush acknowledged this and let them in. They work hard for little money, clean many homes and offices, pick produce, bus dishes, cook and serve millions of meals. They take care of American children, often practically raising them."

"And," said one president, "they pay taxes, every time they buy something. Most of them are model citizens, well, I mean model people. They are honest, hard working and respectful toward others. Sending them home will wreak havoc with our already fragile labor markets."

"Please," the presidents said in unison, "don't deport them. We were loyal to you in your war to the death against Soviet communism in Central America."

"I hear you," said Clinton, "but we're a country of law. Our Congress passed and I signed a new immigration law that cancels our old one. Yes, we're a nation of immigrants, but in the 90's we don't want immigrants any more—especially not poor ones. You see, we no longer have a labor shortage and therefore we don't need the poor and the persecuted immigrants that built our infrastructure and made us a great nation of immigrants."

"I'll make an exception for millionaires because by the new standards they have better characters than those with less money."

The Central American presidents shook their heads. "Some gratitude for our decades of cooperation."

"Hey," Clinton said, painfully rising and hugging each of them. "I feel your pain. I also feel the pain of immigrants facing deportation. I feel the pain of millions of American citizens, whom I tossed off the welfare rolls. But mostly, I have to tell you, I feel the pain in my knee, which hurts like a son of a gun."

Defending the Clintons

May 12, 1997

A friend forwarded to me a couple of recent Hillary Clinton remarks that go a long way toward dispelling the cynicism that has arisen around Clinton's presidency.

In a column that Hillary circulates to lots of newspapers she focused on her husband's deep understanding of suffering. Instead of mocking him when he says things like "I feel your pain," we should take him seriously because since he injured his knee he comprehends pain more viscerally than ever and it has given him a deeper sense of empathy.

For example, Mrs. Clinton described how, thanks to the torn tissue in her husband's knee and his temporary dependence on crutches, he had gained new insight into the struggles that former President Franklin Roosevelt endured with his crippling polio.

Previously, Hillary had imparted to Larry King new and intimate feelings about the nation's first couple's identification with other great people in this world who have also suffered the slings and arrows of outrageous fortune and fate and especially their critics in the media and Congress.

She told King that as she and Bill read the daily barrage leveled against them over the Whitewater scandals, they think of Nelson Mandela and all he had to abide in order to eventually lead his country.

The engineer recording this program just laughed at what I said. No, I'm serious. We have yet to understand the greatness of the Clintons, their capacity to understand the pain and suffering of the world's poor through their own experiences.

You think it's easy for ambitious, middle-class people to lead the greatest country in the history of the world, especially in these troubled times?

Look at the attacks these two well-intentioned people have had to stomach. There was travelgate, Paula Jones and troopergate with tales of Bill's supposedly insatiable sexual appetite. He could also down four Big Macs and two chocolate shakes in one sitting. But he's a growing boy.

Then came the Whitewater loans and shadow around Vince Foster's suicide and the not-talking McDougalls and Web Hubbell and all the hush, I mean, sympathy money he received from Lincoln Bedroom renters. The media made a big deal over John Huang, the Lippo Combine's man with security clearance racing from classified meetings in Commerce to the nearest pay phone. Then the hoopdedoo over campaign contributions from foreigners. Can you imagine having to wake up each morning and read this kind of material?

I feel for our first couple and admire their principles, whatever they are. Because those principles also guide their legal defense strategy.

President Bill refused to turn over supposedly crucial Whitewater notes to the special prosecutor because his lawyers had convinced him that appealing the demand to the Supreme Court was "the right thing to do for America."

That's exactly the kind of patriotic thinking that is taking this nation straight into the 21st Century.

Congo Dance

May 23, 1997

In the 1960s we didn't trust African people to elect their leaders. Why? After independence, the people of the Belgian Congo showed bad judgment. They elected Patrice Lumumba, who wanted the wealth of the Congo to go to its people. Belgium didn't want to see its precious resources wasted on Africans, so they backed a secession movement in Katanga province, where minerals and precious gems were located. Lumumba asked the Soviet Union for help to get it back.

Thus, the Cold War came to the Congo and CIA operatives mounted a coup, threw Lumumba out and, when he threatened to fight back with a nationalist movement, the CIA attempted to assassinate him. But before the CIA hit men got there, the Belgians' puppet in Katanga, Moise Tshombe, captured Lumumba and had him beaten to death.

The CIA then found a guy whom the press labeled a Congolese strong man, a metaphor for "our guy in the Congo." We knew him then as Joseph Mobutu. Now, he's Mobuto Sese Selko, cancer ridden, defeated and fleeing Zaire—which we once knew and will know again as the Congo.

For almost four decades, Mobutu remained our agent. He collected more fees from the CIA than any other agent. And he worked well with our corporations—besides, would you rather have a pro-Soviet African in power? So he knocked his own people around a bit. No one's perfect.

Mobutu allowed Zaire to serve as a base for CIA operations against Angola, whose new government had obtained help from Cuba. Mobutu's brother-in-law, Holden Roberto, got lots of CIA money for running an anti-Angola movement based in Zaire. When the CIA saw Roberto achieving nothing but personal wealth, Mobutu channeled CIA funds to another agent, Jonas Savimbi.

Mobutu didn't believe in sharing his country's wealth with its own people, so he meted out as little as possible to them for medical care, schooling and other services. He kept most for construction projects—like building a large villa in France.

Then the Cold War faded. Neither the U.S. government nor the big companies needed an eyesore in Zaire, like Marcos in the Philippines or Pinochet in Chile. Those loyal friends helped us when we needed them, but the CIA is not sentimental.

The CIA can try to work with Laurent Kabila, the guy Che Guevara had doubts about in the mid 1960s, the guy to whom Stanford University once paid millions in ransom for the release of kidnapped students working with Jane Goodall.

Well, the CIA financed strong man Mobutu. Stanford financed strong man Kabila. Are you optimistic about the future of Zaire, I mean the Republic of the Congo?

My Kingdom for Affirmative Action!

May 23, 1997

After a brief trial, voters of several states and some of our highest courts have decided to scrap affirmative action. The reason: it discriminated against the white majority.

One year after affirmative action ended legally, University of California law schools at Berkeley and UCLA, prohibited from using race as an admission criteria, reported that first-year Hispanic and black entrants had dropped by 80%. The University of Texas at Austin had similar results. Four of five minority applicants that would have gone to law school a year ago didn't meet the current color-blind criteria. As Claude Rains said to Humphrey Bogart in Casablanca upon "discovering" a roulette wheel in Bogie's gambling club, "This is shocking."

It's shocking when *education* President Clinton offers $35 billion in federal funds for middle- and upper-middle-class families who must bear the burden of college tuition—instead of putting that money into reviving sick primary and secondary school education in poor and minority areas.

We didn't need Sherlock Holmes to predict that without affirmative action guidelines for higher education, fewer African-American and Hispanic kids would qualify. Because many receive lousy education from kindergarten on, and given prevailing barrio and ghetto cultures, which hardly foster school learning, those kids need a break.

It's why we initiated affirmative action. Our society has shown an unwillingness to deal with the root cause of racism—because it brings up the uncomfortable issue of class as well. Congress doesn't consider redistributing income—nor integrating housing and thus neighborhoods. So, affirmative action arose, as a minimal form of delayed compensation to a small minority.

It seemed the least we could do. But affirmative action, like all half-hearted attempts to deal with the most discomfort-causing issue in American politics, allowed the rich to continue to avoid having to share some of their wealth with the most hated sector of the poor—who tend to have darker skin color.

For example, most prestigious universities give preference to kids of alumni, especially alumni who contribute to university endowment. Coincidentally, almost all of these former graduates, whose kids get admitted despite low test scores, happen to have the lighter skin persuasion.

This fact should open up government match grant proposal: for every dollar spent by rich white families to insure that their kids get into good universities, the government coughs up a dollar for kids whose families can't afford donations.

The federal grant to poor children from families with income less than $25,000 a year would be applied directly to education and give millions of kids a chance to escape the culture of poverty. It might also get them a ticket into the poverty of culture—American culture, which appeals to consumer desire.

Picture your kid with a Ph.D. quoting King Richard: "My kingdom for a Corvette," instead of "My kingdom for a pair of Air Jordans."

Shocking Army Sexual Behavior

June 11, 1997

The military has generated hot scandals lately. Not over being charged $500 for military toilet seats or the exam cheating at the Naval Academy—not even that The Citadel wouldn't accept women, and when it finally did, treated them brutally. *Sixty Minutes* revealed recently that a Ku Klux Klan-Nazi culture exerts considerable influence on that bastion of southern military tradition. Even the Gulf War syndrome cover-up pales. You recall that the military lied to thousands of troops exposed to chemical weapons and told them their symptoms were psychosomatic.

No, the shock came with the discovery that some of those on whom we've spent considerable money to train as killers, whom we trust to guard our nation's security by dropping tons of nuclear weapons on any of our enemies should they be so ordered, have engaged in dalliance outside the sacred marriage bed. That, we moralists find unacceptable.

First, drill sergeants forced recruits of the opposite sex to give them favors. The whole point of the military is to teach these recruits to kill the enemy without hesitation, rid themselves of human feelings so they can pull a trigger, launch a rocket, drop a bomb without thinking of the death and destruction of those we label as the enemy.

Now, imagine a killer in training, who still possesses enough human feeling to take offense when a drill sergeant abuses her sexually! Quelle scandale!

On top of forced marches and the other physical and mental brutalizations that comprise military education comes the ultimate indignity. Drill sergeants in several military bases actually raped members of the opposite sex. In the good old days they only abused recruits of the same sex.

Then came the culminating shock: some of our military officers have actually gone to bed with married people, and married military officers have consorted with single people. A woman bomber pilot who could have dropped tons of bombs on our

134

potential enemy instead indulged her cravings with a married man—in defiance of orders from her superior to suppress such human urges. And we lose her valuable services as a bomber pilot! Ah! Then a general, a man named to head the Joint Chiefs of Staff, behaved just like a regular citizen by allowing his feelings to translate into the actual sex act outside of the Biblically sacred marriage bed.

What's this country coming to? Let's return to the Bible to regain our clarity. In Exodus Moses received God's commandments, the sixth of which says, "Thou Shalt Not Kill." Then God countermands in Deuteronomy "For the Lord is He that goeth with you, to fight for you against your enemies, to save you." Now, that clears it up. And don't forget, you service men and women, if your libido starts itching, sing the sacred hymn: "Onward Christian soldiers, marching as to war"—not to bed with some yummy of the opposite sex.

Income Gap Widens, But Who Cares?

June 13, 1997

It's possible, the United Nations Development Agency (UNDA) reported on Thursday June 12, to eliminate poverty in the next century. If nations truly aspire to narrow differences between genders and classes, they'll have to change their political ways and their habits for managing global trade and do a little sharing.

Is it worth it? Can we do it? Depends on priorities. For example, the U.S. Congress, in line with the president's thinking, approved a budget that increases military spending by $53 billion over the next five years and simultaneously cuts Medicare by $115 billion and food stamps by $30 billion. The new budget eliminates money to rebuild rotting schools.

Compare that with the words of James Gustave Speth, director of the U.N. Development Program. "Mass poverty is the gravest human tragedy of our time." These reports don't make hot news items like the stock market's hitting a new high yesterday. Yet, the worldwide rich-poor gap has widened as the global economy has expanded. The gains simply bypass millions of people, the United Nations report said. Think of the economic and technological leaps in the last 50 years. Yet, 25% the world's population live in severe poverty; about 33%, 1.3 billion people, survive on less than $1 a day, according to the U.N. Human Development Report.

You like figures? Think of the poorest 20 percent of the world's population earning 1.1 percent of global income in 1996. In 1991 the poorest 20% earned 1.4 percent. In five years, the poorest have suffered a drastic drop in income.

So, who got their share? The UN study says "The greatest benefits of globalization have been garnered by a fortunate few. A rising tide of wealth is supposed to lift all boats, but some are more seaworthy than others ...and some are sinking."

Not only sub-Saharan Africans, northeast Brazilians or rural Cambodians occupy the pits of poverty. Indeed, wealth divisions have increased also in the United States and Britain in recent years, the UN report said. Unemployment in industrialized countries has hit its highest since the 1930s.

What's wrong? World trade and foreign investment have mushroomed. But two-thirds of all foreign direct investment went into eight developing countries. Large population centers, like Russia and Brazil, have slumped badly. Other lagging countries include Iraq, Rwanda, Sudan, Haiti, Jordan and Kenya. The reasons given include the spread of AIDS, crime, war and economic stagnation. The biggest deterioration in the past decade came in eastern Europe, where about a third of the people live on less than $4 a day after the fall of communism, the report said. We won the Cold War.

Our versions of democracy and free market economics prevail in most of the world. What could possibly have gone wrong to explain the horrifying statistics of the UN study? Well, maybe we shouldn't only cut Medicare, food stamps and funds for schools, but our UN dues as well? Who wants to read this kind of bad news on a day when stocks went up?

Polimorals

June 17, 1997

People are tut tutting about the Ruthann Aron case. Police arrested and charged her with conspiring to murder her husband of 30 years, a noted urologist. In addition, police say she had also hatched plans to murder a lawyer who had sued her and another lawyer who had testified against her at a libel trial.

She paid an undercover cop posing as a hit man a down-payment to murder her hubby. In her car, police found assassination manuals, pamphlets on silencers and other incriminating material. This woman ran for the Senate in the 1994 Republican Primary.

"Supposing she had won," my friend said. "Imagine, a murderer representing the people of Maryland!"

"Hold it," I said, "Why single Ruth Aron out of a society filled with callousness? A teenage couple murder their baby in a motel room, another adolescent gives birth at a prom, offs the baby and then goes out to dance the Macarena! A New York City kid who knifes, shoots and robs a teacher, Arthur Levin, and then brags about it."

"You don't see a difference," he said, "between acts of confused teenagers and that of a person that as Senator would have had access to the nation's most vital national security secrets, whose vote on issues could have changed destiny?"

"You mean she would have shared the venue with the great moral characters of our time like Teddy Kennedy and Gus d'Amato? Or Newt Gingrich, the guy who looks like an oversized toddler, but whose idea of ethics is what's mine is mine and what's yours is mine? We've lost our moral compass," I responded.

"Come on," my friend said. "You sound bitter."

"Bitter. As the acerbic comedian said, 'If I was Catholic I would give up hope for Lent.' "

"You're looking only at the down side," he said. "How about seeing the bright side? President Clinton has taken the initiative and raised the race issue as a focus for national debate. The good guys have put it to the tobacco industry. Activists have confronted the triumphant globalizers with facts on child labor and sweat shops. And, the cops did get Ruth Aron before she could realize her wicked her plan. The system works."

I tried to smile. What did Whitewater, Paula Jones, the Indonesian family and other foreign capitalists' payoffs to the Democrats have to do with the larger issues in the world—like global warming, ozone depletion, poverty and hunger among hundreds of millions of people?

"Why," I asked my friend as a parting remark, "do you think people like Ruth Aron become so attracted to politics that she would want to run for the Senate?"

"Oh," he said, "I think it's probably just money and power—you know, the two basic values that make our world turn round. And power doesn't always corrupt, does it?"

Toxic Secret Area 51

July 26, 1997

Area 51—100 miles from Las Vegas, in the midst of a desert. Armed soldiers stand guard as workers unload from trucks the materials used to make Stealth bombers. In this secret air force base, workers then set fire to the toxic material. Coincidentally, these workers have suffered high rates of severe respiratory ailments, cancers, growths and rashes. Some have died. The government denies that anything happens in Area 51. Yet, it prohibits those who work there from speaking about their work. Area 51 is funded through the secret security budget.

Victims and their families have filed suit against the government, but courts have upheld the government's claim that the material is too sensitive to release: national security.

We have a war on drugs, campaigns against drunk driving and tobacco advertising. Why not a movement to stop the government from hiding crimes behind a dangerous holdover from the past: national security?

When government officials speak those two words, parades of horror ensue. From the 1940s on, the government used national security guidelines to withhold health data on low level radiation dangers in areas near the above-ground atomic tests. Lots of down-winders got cancer. Soldiers, used as guinea pigs, suffered similar ailments. A couple of ghouls, called doctors, in Cincinnati General Hospital, zapped cancer patients with whole body radiation—so the Pentagon could discover how people react to nuclear exposure in battlefield situations.

One nuclear gangster admitted to me that the Soviets knew all about the dangers of nuclear radiation to human health. The data remained classified—not from the Soviet Union, but from our own people.

The Atomic Energy Commission told the public not to fear nuclear fallout when the commissioners knew full well that a great menace existed. But if the public knew the risks of continued nuclear testing, they might have shut down the nuclear project.

Then there's the FBI, which routinely violated the Constitution because national security required they intrude on people's private lives. National security has justified lies, cover-ups, coups and secret wars. Mossadegh and Arbenz, the leaders of Iran and Guatemala, knew about the CIA's supposedly hidden hand in the coups of 1953 and 1954. The CIA kept the information from the U.S. public, because conspiring to overthrow a legal government violates U.S. law, as did CIA-backed assassination attempts, or the Agency's sponsorship of the secret wars needed to battle the evil empire. The Cold War, of course, transcended the Constitution.

Now, we learn that under the guise of national security secrecy the government has people burning toxic waste. The victims have sued, not for money but to force the government to admit the truth and apologize. No way, say the national security officials who, like drunken drivers and typhoid Marys, march relentlessly on—even though there's no longer an enemy to justify withholding the material. Anyone out there want to organize to force logic and truth to the surface and banish those two words, "national security," from government vocabulary? No more secrets and lies!

Tobacco Companies Have Reformed?

August 12, 1997

I listen to Rush Limbaugh on AM radio here in Santa Cruz, California. Don't worry, I haven't converted—yet.

Rush thinks that the campaign against the tobacco companies amounts to yet another liberal plot to deprive Americans of basic individual rights.

The cigarette makers have already made concessions, he explains to his audience of mega-ditto heads. They've offered billions to settle the claims and, what's most important, they've stopped targeting kids in their ads and concentrate totally on adults—especially foreigners who don't have to put up with that crap about smoking causing cancer, heart disease, emphysema, etc.

Then, I read an upsetting story in the August 8 *San Jose Mercury News* that says the Tobacco Control Coalition, a community organization, conducted a survey of almost 400 stores, over 20% of the retail establishments in Santa Clara County. Surprise! The surveyors discovered an average of 34 tobacco ads per store throughout this Silicon Valley area—the same as in 1995 when they conducted their first survey. So, in three years of promising to not target kids, the tobacco companies have lied. Shocking!

The ads imply: smoke and you'll have fun, get good sex, have nice clothes and fancy cars. In short, smoking is really cool. Beautiful people stare at each other the way teenagers long to be looked at—Newport Pleasure. And if you want to be a super macho man, even without Joe, smoke a camel. The chicks will definitely respond to such a virile male act.

Rush might say that there's no proof about kid targeting. Well, the surveyors found that the tobacco companies placed about one third of the ads near candy counters. Almost 50 percent were displayed below the height of three feet—and there aren't that many size disadvantaged adults in Santa Clara County.

Limbaugh tends to dismiss unpleasant facts, but stores within 1000 feet of schools had a significantly higher number of tobacco ads. Liquor stores, chain supermarkets and chain convenience stores all contained high numbers of pro smoke ads.

In Santa Clara, concerned citizens talked to store owners and succeeded in getting some to remove or limit the ads.

But before Congress cuts any deal with the criminals who call themselves tobacco CEOs, they ought to insert a clause that eliminates tobacco advertising. I'd prefer Nuremberg Trials, but I'll settle for a larger payment to the public and a new ad that's aimed at kids and teenagers: It would show a kid in a hospital badly coughing. Camera zooms in on his pain-wracked face.

"It was worth it. Smoking helped me get attention," he says. "My parents act nicer to me now that I'm dying." He hacks an oyster into the bed spittoon. "So, if you want more parental attention, smoke away, kids."

Dioxin in School Chickens and More

August 18, 1997

"Traces of toxin found in L.A. schools' chicken," the headline screams. The August 17 *Associated Press* report says that Los Angeles school kids had already consumed most of the 77 cases of dioxin-tainted chickens. Federal officials downplayed the idea that a little dioxin could hurt anyone. "A very low level of dioxin," said Margaret Webb, spokeswoman for the Food Safety and Inspection Service of the U.S. Department of Agriculture.

U.S. officials admit they know little about the effects on humans of dioxin, an industrial by-product. Nevertheless, the FDA raised the acceptable level of dioxin in meat from 1 part per trillion to 4 parts per trillion—whatever that means.

Government investigators discovered that the chicken company had mixed dioxin-contaminated clay mined in Mississippi with chicken feed. Not to worry, says the FDA, that feed has been destroyed.

The government ranked this dioxin-chicken scare below last spring's school panic when students from several states ate strawberries tainted with hepatitis.

My ten-year-old starts school in Los Angeles County in two weeks. How do parents respond to a company sending 650 cases of possibly poisonous chicken to the LA Unified School District—for consumption by the kids?

This follows the story of the Arkansas-based Hudson Meat Packing Company shipping a million pounds of hamburger possibly containing e-coli bacteria. Zounds!

Remember the alar scare, the impure apple juice episode, the orange juice contamination?

Combine this with recent revelations that the government lied to the public about the extent of strontium 90 and other radioactive material in milk supplies. The nuclear ghouls carried out their atomic tests without regard to consequences for the environment. Cows ate fallout-laden grasses and passed the radioactive material on to nursing mothers and children.

Does this panic you? Does one seek a remote South Pacific island on which to grow one's own food and eat fresh fish from the pristine ocean?

"No", says a doctor friend. "First, fish everywhere contain high mercury levels because of the crap that industry has poured into the ocean. Then, the government tested hundreds of atomic bombs over Pacific Ocean islands. Also, from the late 1940s into the early 1970s, the government dumped into the oceans nuclear waste stored in barrels. Some barrels began leaking radioactive goo, which entered the food chain. No safe place to run."

"OK," I said, regaining my composure. "What do you do about a situation where one must worry about eating hamburger, chicken, strawberries, fish—or drinking milk."

"Don't forget smog," he laughed. "Well, check your garden soil for poisons, grow your own veggies, make your kids' lunch. Congress could help citizens to file law suits against companies that send out tainted food."

Of course, that would mean we'd have to elect a different Congress next year.

Sex Distracts!

August 26, 1997

Achieving celebrity status means revealing your sex life. Americans and British in particular seem to share an unlimited interest in the genital activities of the rich and famous. "But," I ask my friend who writes for one of the exposé tabloids, "why should people get excited because actor Hugh Grant paid for what Paula Jones says Bill Clinton wanted from her."

"Because we know Grant from the movies as this innocent and charming young man, not a jaded, oversexed roué."

"But doesn't it become stale?" I asked. "In recent months we've learned that Marv Albert, the dramatic voice that delivers professional basketball on the radio and TV, got so excited that he bit a woman (not his wife) in a motel room. Frank "Cleancut" Gifford, as boring of voice as Albert is dynamic, also consummated his lust with a woman other than Kathie Lee. Lt. Kelly Flynn, a B-52 pilot, had sexual urges that took her into a married man's bed—proving I suppose that libidinous activities occur even in the lives of trained killers. Is that a good reason for court-martialing her?"

"No," he replied, "but it makes for great feature stories. And don't forget the Kennedy boys—from '30-second-Jack' to 'rape-'em-if-you-can-Willie-Smith' and 'get-'em-under-age-Michael.'

"But look at stories we missed," he said. "Former FBI Director J. Edgar Hoover collected sex data on Martin Luther King, Jr."

"Well, if lots of people behave in kinky ways, why should it make headlines?" I inquired. "Why focus on the sex lives of other people and not, for example, on equally taboo bathroom habits. You don't read invented stories even in the tabloids."

"Let's face it," he said, "lots of Americans have kinky thoughts, but don't dare act on them."

"But," I said, "that's irresponsible. Why should Anthony Quinn's abusive behavior years ago make the newspapers today? To make his kids suffer?"

"Hey," he said. "Prurient interest has no time limit! The churches tell us how we're supposed to behave and it's news when our role models didn't or don't conform to those standards. Tens of millions of fundamentalists continue to hold onto those mores, just so they can assure themselves that they're sinners—and not enjoy their sins."

"Also," he added, "staying interested in other people's sex lives, celebrities' or your neighbors', will distract you from peripheral issues like politics. So, remember the rumor that Zazie is divorcing Googie to marry Boobie, who made millions in the emu egg trade—not who gets what from the national budget and how the corporate elite rip you off each day."

Stop the Weapons Madness and Ask Reasonable Questions

September 2, 1997

Before voting on military budgets and expanding moribund alliances, Members of Congress need to pose the question: what is the purpose of the immense U.S. military machine in alliance with dozens of others in an era where there are no apparent enemies? This question also pertains to weapons sales at home and abroad. Why, for example, do South American nations with vast numbers of their population living in sub-poverty conditions need to have U.S.-made F-16 fighters in their air forces?

Similarly, why do nations recently emerging from the Soviet bloc require sophisticated weapons at the very time when Russia, their supposed enemy, can no longer field a viable army, navy or air force? Indeed, expanding NATO and rearming Poland, Hungary and Czechoslovakia could turn into a provocative operation against a Russian giant whose only defense will be her nuclear arsenal. Unless, of course, some genius defense intellectual designs a plan to include Russia in NATO, so they too can buy useless weapons.

Behind this fervor for expansion of military alliances in the name of "making the world safe" lies the expansion of what has become the transnational weapons conglomerates. As the June 14, 1997 *Economist* illustrated, the weapons industry has, like most other sectors of the economy, turned into a transnational oligopoly. Mergers and consolidations have brought about the consolidation of major giants like Boeing with McDonnell-Douglas. Boeing received most of its revenues from sales of civilian aircraft; McDonnell-Douglas from military planes.

Similarly, European monster conglomerates will cooperate with the American giants to produce a single military plane for the future—just in case an enemy might emerge. Following the globalization trend, parts for these modern military aircraft and hi tech weapons, like parts for capital goods, are manufactured in other countries, where labor is less expensive. Indeed, China plays a role in some weapons systems and, of course, is eager to get advanced western weapons technology. The Chinese market is still a possibility in the eyes of some far-sighted arms salesmen.

But the big "defense contractors" see the inclusion of new eastern European nations into the North Atlantic Treaty Organization as an immediate way to ensure the enlargement of their markets. By including ever more countries in an alliance against nobody, the defense business will boom. An F-16, which the United States will sell to the new NATO countries and some South American aspirants, costs $30 million per plane. The F-22, the future jet fighter, will go for $100 million a pop.

More than sixty years ago, the Nye Committee discovered that arms makers had pushed extra hard and not quite ethically to induce public opinion and Congress to favor a declaration of war that led to U.S. involvement in World War I. Should Congress investigate their role today, they would discover that what President Eisenhower called the "military industrial complex" has lost none of its power; if anything, it has gained strength. Its new project, pushing for NATO expansion, feeds right into its business plans. The future, the weapons company CEOs believe, looks very bright. Last year three "defense" companies, Lockheed Martin, Boeing/McDonnell-Douglas and Raytheon/Hughes/Texas Instruments had a combined revenue from military sales of some $50 billion. Less than ten other U.S. firms sold more than $15 billion in high tech weapons. To fight against terrorists? Drug traffickers?

The arms tycoons promote weapons sales as means of reinforcing peaceful alliances. In this Orwellian world where colonels and generals don't retire and then fade away, but become VIPs in the defense industry, the more armaments that we sell, the more chances there are for world peace. In addition to promoting NATO expansion, the military industrial moguls see weapons sales as a way to promote friendship with South Korea, Taiwan and Japan.

Over 11 million people work directly in defense production, not counting sales and maintenance personnel and millions more relate indirectly to the war economy. This is a reduction of 6 million in the last ten years. The high tech weaponry has consumed an ever greater share of the military budget. The companies helped the Pentagon and the television "news" producers to design the Gulf War show, where the public watched the new state of the art bombs, missiles and electronic guidance systems carry out a technological massacre on TV.

The future calls for less manpower and more sci-fi weapons, which will literally have no earthly use. In 1996, global military spending reached close to a trillion dollars, with the United States doing the lion's share. What might it have come to if we had an enemy?

Saul Landau

Campaign Financing Means Free Speech

September 9, 1997

Have you listened to the campaign finance hearings? The vice president forgot, the Buddhists didn't realize, and Mr. Fowler, the Democratic National Committee chief maven, suffers from selective amnesia. In his eagerness to collect election money, he forgot conversations with CIA officials, in which the president's team attempted to obtain kosher stamps for shady foreign businessmen.

Mr. Fowler talked about principles: in a democracy, people who contribute money should have access to power. Why, the Supreme Court has equated campaign financing with free speech. Freedom means nothing if not a chance to share your business problems with the president, in case he might have ideas about how to make more profits for you.

Picture the following scenario.

Mr. Gus Downandout has lived across the street from the White House for years, in Lafayette Park. By noon he has panhandled $1.19. He washes his face in the Union Station bathroom, before the surveillance cops can 86 him, puts scotch tape over holes in trousers and shirt, runs his gritty nails through his matted hair and marches into the DNC office.

"Pew," says the receptionist, "what do you want?"

"I'm contributing to the DNC," says Gus, throwing his change down on her desk.

She calls her superior.

"What can I do for you, er, sir?" the young DNC staffer asks.

"I want to see the president," says Gus. "I need help, like all the other homeless people. I heard that by contributing money, citizens get access to power. So, here's my money. When do I see Clinton—or if not him I'll settle for Hillary."

Several staffers assembled and, trying not to hold their noses, they began to push Gus toward the door.

"Stop," he shouted. "What if I told you that I'm a billionaire in disguise, just testing your principles. Now that I see who you are, I'm going to give my money to the Republicans. They won't care how a person dresses or how often he bathes—as long as he's got money for the next election."

"This guy might be for real," said one DNCer. "Remember those poor-looking Buddhists who contributed oodles? Call Fowler. Have a seat Mr. Whatever-Your-Name-Is. Want a cup of coffee, a donut?"

"You know," he said, putting the $1.19 back into his greasy pocket, "I understand the link between speech and money now."

"Huh?" said one the staffers.

"Money is free speech," he said. "If you got one, you get the other. But some folks are so greedy that the mere mention of money changes their behavior."

"Well," he said as he exited, "good luck. And by the way, your donuts are soggy and your coffee is weak. And tell Al Gore hello from one of the guys who used to wear the yellow robe."

Saul Landau

Virtual Suicide

September 24, 1997

I read this morning that Bobby, an eleven-year-old boy, had hung himself by his bathrobe belt from a bathroom fixture. The boy's parents and paramedics tried desperately but in vain to revive him.

Bobby had received an email rejection letter from a twelve-year-old girl, with whom he had established an electronic mail correspondence. He left no suicide note—nothing but the back-up copies of his internet messages, ending in that last casual touch of the send key on the rejecting girl's keyboard.

When those burning bites appeared on his monitor, saying, "don't write me anymore," the boy fell into virtual despair, and decided that his virtual love life was over and real life was not worth living without the regular messages from his electronic sweetheart. Does this indicate that virtual rejection stings as painfully as the real thing, that a Dear John letter inside the computerized world arouses the same responses as a face-to-face kiss-off used to?

At the Ontario Mills Mall, the virtual reality parlor draws more people than any other of the amusement centers—including the IMAX 3D theater, where you can dive to the bottom of the sea and watch from an inch away as a moray attempts to devour an octopus. You can buy virtual experiences that last a minute or two: motorcycle racing, deep sea fishing and ski jumping—without ever having to leave your chair.

It doesn't require a leap of imagination to place yourself in the world of virtual sex—the logical sequel to virtual love. Imagine a way to access the playgirl or playboy of the month on the internet, with audio to accompany the 3D picture, and a texture simulator that, when applied to body parts, imitates the touch of a person of the same or opposite sex. And there's no emotional problems—not even the possibility of a real person writing a rejection letter on the virtual communication wave lengths.

May little Bobby's suicide induce scientists and technicians to ever greater virtual heights, so that every form of human need can be satisfied without ever having to deal with another human being—which can be such a problem.

And to bring you back to real earth, imagine how the very report of this commentary will lead to a jump in stock price of Virtual Realities Inc. and other companies who have invested in the virtual future. With virtualism ruling the world, there is no end to downsizing of the labor supply, with the resulting increase in profits. Capitalism—what a wonderful system. If only we could make it virtual! We could then revive poor little Bobby.

Saul Landau

Fast Track: God's Lane

October 7, 1997

President Clinton wants Congress to provide him with Fast Track legislation, a means to sign up new NAFTA partners, without having Congress meddling in the details of trade. After almost four years of NAFTA, the free trade agreement with our North American friends and neighbors, Canada and Mexico, it's time to look at some results. My pro-NAFTA friend glowed: "Look at the thousands of new factories that have arisen in Mexico, on our border, where they're so convenient. What a boon for the border economy."

"How about the environmental mess that has spread because of industry?" I asked. "Rivers, land, air, have gone to hell and, even more perfidious, the governments have spent almost no money to clean up the mess."

"A fund exists for the cleanup," he replied coldly.

"Yes," I replied, "Even though Clinton promised, he's done diddly squat, spent no money to right the wrongs done to Nature as a result of the rights granted to trade."

"President Clinton is the Franklin Roosevelt of our age, " he said. "Clinton's given us the New Deal for trade. What FDR did for labor, give 'em hope, Clinton's done for CEOs of major transnational enterprises."

"What's more important?" he asked, "Jobs, better wages than they used to get, a booming economy, or a little damage done to soil, water and air—which our technicians and scientists will clean up, as soon as they figure out how."

"But," I said, trying to keep my temper, "think of the thousands of people who have been affected by toxic dumping into the air, water and soil. If they and their children die prematurely from the effects of environmental contamination, they won't enjoy benefits derived from jobs."

"What are you, some kind of sentimental tree hugger, whale wussy? Your ideas stand in the way of the future, where every illiterate African kid could own his own laptop, every Chinese family could own at least one car and maybe a speedboat, where developers cover the world's undeveloped areas with eight lane highways and undiscovered beaches have Club Med resorts."

"So," I said, "you probably don't care much about labor rights either."

"I honor labor," he stiffened. "But I don't think they need coddling by Congress examining minor instances of starvation wages or child labor, or minor infractions of toxic dumping. Let's move to the 21st century where everyone will accept the free market as God's will, where buying and selling becomes the highest interaction between people. Let's stop this sentimental crap about labor rights, environment, border cleanup. Fast Track means more worthy nations will enter NAFTA and free trade, God's way, will advance."

"You're right," I said. "Stop this sentimental crap about rights and environment and we may watch God playing dice with the cosmos."

Saul Landau

Saddam and Don King

October 17, 1997

Following is an interview with a man claiming he's Don King:

"You represent Saddam Hussein?"

"You mean, the great heavyweight contender of 1991, now making a comeback?"

"I mean the President of Iraq."

"That man from central casting? He made his first TV appearance as a heavy in the 1970s as leader of the Baath party—we called it blood bath party cause they killed so many of their enemies, and even some of their own members. What a career, from fifteenth ranking flyweight to heavyweight challenger—a reputation so bad that he got to duke it out with the champion, George 'Low Blow' Bush. Now, even after that humiliating loss, he's got a possible rematch with reigning champ, 'Slick Willie' Clinton."

"You sound like a boxing promoter."

"Hey, I promote anything. Saddam was a challenge. People don't remember, but during the 1980s series of matches with Iran, Washington gave him military intelligence on Iran's weakness. It's not easy to turn a buddy into an enemy and have the public believe it! U.S. Ambassador to Iraq, April Glaspie, admitted that she told Saddam that if he wanted to punch Kuwait's lights out, it wasn't our business. She said that just as Saddam cocked his right fist to hit them royal Kuwaiti SOBs."

"But in the 1991 Gulf War, the U.S. and UN forces devastated Iraq, killed civilians, destroyed sewage treatment plants, humbled its military…"

"Hey, their military was always humble. You believed that hype about the invincible republican guard, Saddam having the fourth largest army in the world, the accuracy of scud missiles? Did the public ever buy that sell job! The TV audience for that fight was the largest ever in fighting history."

"You mean the current story about Iraq making biological, chemical and nuclear weapons is hype?"

"I didn't say that. Saddam, like any other fighter in that region, has real enemies. Iran, Israel, Turkey. They already have those weapons and worse. And if threatened by them, Saddam might use those weapons. But not against us. Remember in the Technological Massacre, I mean Gulf War, U.S. artillery, not Saddam's, blew up chemical weapons storage plants and exposed Americans to Gulf War disease."

"The United States has promised 'dire consequences.' "

"Not all U.S. partners buy that line. Remember this. Saddam still has a contract with central casting."

"Huh?"

"Ask 'Low Blow' Bush and 'Slick Willie''s managers about that. I hear Saddam signed a ten-year contract as black hat in TV productions. He's got a few years left. He lost the Gulf fight, but the body blows landed on the Iraqi people and their infrastructure. Bush never laid a glove on Saddam himself. Part of the contract."

"Hmn," I said. "I wonder."

Saul Landau

Intolerant Jewish Stomachs versus McDonald's

October 22, 1997

When I was kid, my grandmother warned me not to eat pork—first, it wasn't kosher and therefore constituted some kind of terrible sin. Worse, she warned, pork could poison a tender stomach with trichinosis. She told of tapeworms that grew out of pig meat that could grow to a thousand feet inside my intestines. My father simply said: "if you eat clams, oysters or any shellfish, you'll die."

"But Daddy," I would say, "lots of people eat them and don't die."

"They're not Jewish," he would reply.

"What difference does that make?" I would naively ask.

"Jewish stomachs can't tolerate that kind of food."

To emphasize the importance of careful food selection, my mother bought me a copy of Upton Sinclair's *The Jungle*, so I could understand the barbaric and unsanitary slaughterhouses— the conditions under which meat was prepared for non-kosher Americans.

But, being a defiant kid at sixteen, I tried oysters, with Tabasco sauce and horseradish, washed down by a cold beer — bought for me by an older guy at the next table.

And I ate other forbidden food: T bones at greasy spoons, ham and eggs and BLT's on toast at diners, and exotic dripping - with-fat pork sausages from street venders. I didn't die or get a terrible stomach ailment; I actually grew taller and gained weight—the eternal concern of my mother.

After all, I maturely reasoned with myself, President Roosevelt and Mayor LaGuardia, my government, would not let irresponsible restaurateurs operate, even street peddlers selling stale hot dogs from their push carts. I grew to love my lobsters, shrimp, crayfish—and even graduated to sushi. So much for those old-fashioned food fears.

But time went by and stories began to appear about fish containing mercury and other dangerous ingredients. Then, recently, came reports that 70% of the chickens you buy, cut into pieces or already cooked at supermarkets and fast food outlets, contain dangerous bacteria—germs that have made millions of people sick and, when not properly cooked, killed some folks.

And over the last six months, meat producers recalled millions of pounds of ground beef because of the presence of E. coli bacteria. "Look," I tell my 11-year-old girl, "no more meals at McDonald's, Burger King or other fast food places. "Here, read this," I say, slamming down a scary salmonella newspaper story, as she dips her Big Mac into a puddle of ketchup.

For her birthday, I bought her a copy of *The Jungle* and subscriptions to organic food magazines that detail the consequences of eating chemically sprayed food. I warn her of the dire consequences of eating the wrong food at the wrong places.

"Wait a second," I tell myself, as I see my 11-year-old sneaking into McDonald's at the Mall, "what am I doing—or was my grandmother right?"

Saul Landau

La Mordida

November 5, 1997

A White House insider passed me the following transcript of one of the videotapes, after a lip reader had deciphered it.

UNIDENTIFIED MALE (UM): Wow, so this is the Lincoln bedroom.

CLINTON: Yes, my good friend, this is the place where worthy presidential guests have slept for more than a century. And let me assure you that your genorosity during this campaign entitles you to spend a night here with your wife—or, er, friend. Well, you know what I mean.

UM: Thank you, Mr. President. Can I call you that? Let me get right to the point. I'm in little girls' underwear and in order to compete in the modern world market, where lots of people want to get into little girls' underwear, we need some special consideration.

CLINTON: Of course, I already sympathize with your plight.

UM: We've already moved our little girls' underwear factory to Mexico. I've taught my managers how to say in Spanish "throw the toxic waste in the river" and "you're fired, you damned union organizer," but I need a little help from the source of power to keep me competitive in little girls' underwear.

CLINTON: (Looking down at notes to see how much contributor actually gave) Hmn, I think that might be possible. What kind of help do you need—and I must tell you, this might cost a little extra.

UM: (taking out checkbook and starting to write) No problem, Bill, can I call you that? You see, you probably don't know that when you do business in Mexico you have to pay people off. They call it *"la mordida"* there. Sometimes, Mexican government officials get a little greedy and, frankly, they keep upping the ante. I thought that maybe a word from you to the Mexican president would help keep their appetites under control, so that I could remain competitive in...

CLINTON: Little girls' underwear, yes, I know (glancing approvingly at size of check). Well, I understand and I think we might be able to do something about your problem.

UM: Thank you, Willy, can I call you that? In this country we know how to do business honestly and express our political beliefs in a pure and sincere manner.

(The two shake hands as tape goes blurry.)

Saul Landau

Global Warming and Character

December 2, 1997

Ibsen's 19th Century play, *An Enemy of the People*, takes place in a town where the economy depends on mineral baths. But the water contains harmful bacteria that eventually kills people who bath in it.

Sacrifice the town's economy by revealing the secret of the poisoned bath waters or conceal it so that the town's economy can survive? The truth teller costs the town its basic industry and he thus becomes an enemy of the people.

In Peter Benchley's 1970's book *Jaws*, a courageous sheriff tries to alert the public that a killer shark feeds on tourists off the town's beach. In each story a hero who challenges the economic establishment. Public health and the economy find themselves at odds.

Flash forward to Kyoto, where world leaders meet to stem the tide of the earth's escalating temperature, while not endangering the very economy that has produced the pattern of global warming. In ten days time, all the nations should agree to change their polluting ways and sign an international accord to prevent global warming.

A piece of logical cake. Every nation should say: "OK, we'll reduce our emissions and make necessary economic adjustments." For example, in China pollution causes one out of every eight deaths. Similar figures exist in Indonesia and other Asian miracle growth economies.

But instead of recognizing the horrors of the development process, the leaders of these nations say to the U.S. and Europe: "You guys did it. Now it's our turn. And besides, the U.S. is still the world's biggest polluter."

We have championed development as God's chosen route to progress and happiness. But the Global Warming Devil has arisen from the smoke stacks, the tail pipes and even the plastics that Santa brings our kids. Our industries, transportation and

163

consumption patterns do more to change the nature of the earth's climate than most of the rest of the nations combined.

We want other countries to consume our products—including cars, trucks, tanks, commercial and military jet planes—and tobacco. What a dilemma. Where is the hero à la *Jaws* or *Enemy of the People*? Will Al Gore say, "Do the right thing, no matter the cost to our economies"? Demonstrating his staunch character, will he say, "We will show the world by dramatically reducing our emissions and press other big polluters like China and Indonesia to do the same—or we won't let them into the juicy trade agreements"?

Don't you feel as confident as I do that the men in the White House will show courage, as they did on welfare and land mines, for example, and do the right thing—even it means bucking establishment donors who contributed lavishly to their campaigns?

Hey, who called me naive?

Saul Landau

World Hunger
Amidst Economic Boom

December 23, 1997

In 1997, while many Americans enjoyed a booming economy, world hunger worsened. A newly-released John Hopkins
University study claims that 18 million people die annually of
starvation or causes related to malnutrition. According to United
Nations statistics, an additional 800 million people suffer from
chronic undernourishment—meaning they consume less than
2200 calories per day. In Haiti, Sub-Saharan Africa or Afghanistan
people's daily food intake falls far below the minimum. Indeed,
in Peru, Surinam, and even in next-door Mexico, millions suffer
from hunger and serious malnutrition.

Over two decades ago delegates to the 1974 Rome food
summit set their goal for abolishing world hunger in a decade.
These optimists believed that science and technology could solve
the food supply problems. They reasoned that through high-yield
varieties of wheat and rice, a veritable "green revolution," science could assure production of adequate food for everyone.

Critics, however, warned that "green revolution" technology alone could not achieve the ambitious task of ensuring food
for all—that food distribution policy must change as well. The
great banks and their partners in agri-business never warmed to
notions of sharing their marketable food with the needy, nor did
they cotton to ideas of nations having programs to meet their
own needs: national food self-sufficiency.

Such policies interfered with agri-business exports, no matter how many people went hungry or even starved as a result. In
Mexico, Egypt, Jamaica and elsewhere, governments fostered
import substitution. Whether or not these programs would have
in fact yielded sufficient food production we do not know
because they did not survive the withering attacks of multi lat-
eral lending agencies and sometimes the CIA.

The technology, however, worked well. More food is now
produced; but more are also hungry. And few look to technology

to overcome structural problems operating inside the global economy.

But the experts have grown more prudent in their goal setting. Last year's food summit called for halving the number of chronically hungry people over twenty years—to only 400 million.

Who would have expected Fidel Castro to stand up and challenge this goal as immoral?"The very modesty of these goals is shameful," said Fidel Castro, when he rose to speak last year in Rome. "The world," he said, "has enough food to feed everyone. So, why should even one person starve, why should one child go hungry?"

It shouldn't have taken Fidel to point out the obvious to the assembled delegates. Hunger accompanies poverty, unequal distribution of wealth. "The rich do not know hunger," Castro said, as he criticized the "offensive opulence and squandering of consumer societies."

Ironically, as the New Year unfolds, celebrants of the free market point precisely to the massive displays of junk that the world economy produces and sells. But the spillover effects of free market go beyond whether or not one appreciates the trinket-casino economy. Under the free market pretext, agro-giants have gained access to markets that previously relied on local producers, often state-subsidized, but also reliable.

Under the free market model, many of these farmers had to abandon the land and seek low-wage work in mass-production industries.

Few of these displaced people read the food sections of the *Washington Post* or *New York Times* that offer sumptuous recipes for the holiday season. Likewise, those who still remain on the infertile land that the green revolution doesn't touch don't belong to the world of holiday feasts and shopping sprees.

Don't feel guilty about enjoying yourselves—well, not too guilty. The American consumer doesn't cause others to suffer. Nor do the victims of our "induced consumption" models foist inequitable distribution of wealth on the world. American consumers didn't make the world food policies, in the name of free market, that have not allowed for some just distribution of food.

So, when you make your resolution, after you've overdosed on eggnog, turkey and pumpkin pie, think of joining or contributing to organizations that approach world hunger problems with clear and doable ideas

Or resolve to write letters to Congress and the Clinton Administration that has helped push free market down the throats of third world people—instead of food.

Cuban Revolution—
Thirty-Nine Years Later

January 5, 1998

Once again the Guiness Book of Records opens its pages to the Cuban Revolution and Fidel Castro. Never in western hemisphere history has a case of such blatant disobedience gone without rectification—by the empire that is.

Secretary of State Madeline Albright ridicules Fidel as a dinosaur. But for much of the world he has emerged as an elder statesman, a hero precisely because he has successfully defied nine consecutive U.S. presidents, all of whom have tried to get rid of him. Moreover, when Fidel appears at international fora like the world food meeting at Rome or on the environment in Rio, he, not the powerful U.S. delegate, receives a standing ovation.

At home, Castro presides over a sick economy. The once-mighty revolution has taken serious body blows. When the Soviet Union collapsed, Cuba lost its sugar daddy. The economy appeared headed down the slippery slope of destruction until 1996, when Cuba posted a substantial growth rate.

But foreign tourism has unfortunately become the new mainstay of the Cuban economy. Indeed, as a foreign exchange earner, it has surpassed sugar. And with tourism, prostitution returned, along with the dreaded lure of consumerism that Castro had fought so hard to keep out.

Castro revived the image of Che Guevara—the humble, austere revolutionary who cared for his fellow beings, not for himself—while simultaneously tourists brought dollars to Cuba. And with them came inequality of income—the very disease that the revolution had so steadfastly opposed.

Castro made these concessions to necessity, but held fast before submitting the Cuban labor force and Cuba's resources to foreign investors. And so, in 1998, Cuba has little foreign capital to work with, thanks in part to the Helms-Burton Act, which threatens outside investors with heavy penalties, but also because

Cuba has refused to make the kinds of concessions that the big companies desire in developing nations.

In 1998, the Cuban Revolution limps along. Its once-fabled health care and education systems remain intact, albeit battered by serious shortages. Cubans still receive modest state subsidies in health, food, housing and child care, whereas in the rest of the world these programs have mostly vanished before the onslaught of the free market and its ruthless ideology.

On January 21, Pope John Paul II is due to arrive, which will mean an enormous boost in Castro's international prestige. He will criticize Cuba's failings on procedural human rights, but the pope, like Fidel, thinks modern capitalism is cruel and unjust. He agrees with Fidel that the opulence and consumer squandering in the face of world hunger and massive poverty is unseemly, that consumerism does not mix well with spirituality.

In March of last year I expressed my pessimism to Fidel. He stared at me and said: "a revolutionary always has hope." It's a good motto with which to start the new year.

Nature Teaches Humility

January 12, 1998

This year Californians suffered flooding instead of earthquakes. One Malibu friend dreamed of being a kid descending an enormous slide into a turbulent pool. Actually, his neighbors had to abandon their homes because of mudslide danger.

Recently, tornadoes decimated towns in Georgia and Kentucky. Maine underwent a horrendous ice storm. The ubiquitous El Niño at work?

Compare these experiences to The Enlightenment lessons we learned about Man dominating Nature by applying Reason and Science to meet its challenges. Somehow, Nature's power eludes our technology—as southern Californians know all too well.

I lay my head on the pillow, proud of having navigated sixty miles on a crowded freeway at high speeds—ah, the power of the automobile. I dream that the house is shaking, that our wine glasses are falling from the shelves. I sit up. The bed room is doing the shimmy shammy. The electricity fails. I turn on the walkman radio. Yes, technology can outwit Nature.

The news reports an earthquake. And expect aftershocks!

I return to my reveries. I am Captain Ahab chasing the White Whale, who assumes the shape of a fearsome looking woman with giant fists that bang into the prow of my ship.

"I warn you," says the whale-woman. "Your ambition and greed exceed your power and ability."

The owners of the ship sit in large offices in a tall building. They do not hear her.

The giant whale creature scoops up an enormous piece of land—shaped like Florida—and blows on it: a hurricane, uprooting trees, detaching the roofs of houses. Still the well-dressed men in the bank office hear and see nothing. The creature grows angry and begins to smash my ship to pieces.

The sailors fall into the sea.

One of the men in the boardroom calmly places his hand on the ship's steering wheel. "I'll take over, Ishmael," he says. He dispatches rescue units to save the drowning men, but a helicopter gets caught in the high winds and falls into the ocean. I hear TV news reporting the story on my walkman as I clutch a rubber tube for survival. I close my eyes and see cars filling freeways, the dams redirecting the flow of rivers, developers planning vast new housing tracts and shopping malls in the desert. The giant creature pulls my face close to hers and commands me to tell the others about the frailty of technology's efforts to control her.

The creature warns me: "I shall return again and again until you understand the lesson." She dives under the sea.

"Beware the hidden hand," I shout. "Nature is a woman," I explain. "Isn't it obvious that she needs nurturing?"

But who is listening?

Zipper-gate: the Death of Politics

January 26, 1998

When the Soviet Union collapsed, Francis Fukiyama, a conservative writer, declared "the end of history": class struggle no longer had relevance. Soviet power meant the hammer and sickle; the International; ideology of working class unity, no matter the nationality. All this collapsed.

History, the working out of that class conflict, had ended. This didn't mean workers would love their bosses, but that the market would determine class relations. The strongest capitalists would control the market. God intended the United States to lead this process.

The president's job was to deregulate, cut government services and privatize everything. The first presiding figure for this new order was William Jefferson Clinton.

Then came zipper-gate, a product of two forces: Clinton's insatiable sex drive and the rebirth in Washington of the 19th Century Russian Inspector General.

The human sex drive remained intact, in this globally harmonious world, and not yet controlled by market force. So, as circumstances indicate, our president indulged himself—only to find relief, of course.

Enter another innate human force: rivalry. Mean-spirited Republicans resented Clinton's ability to indulge himself with members of the opposite sex and get away with it. Having pleasure and not paying a price for it—disgusting! Especially for your rivals.

A sizable Puritan element agreed. Special Prosecutor Kenneth Starr had discovered the Achilles heel of the presidency. Twenty-four-year-old Monica Lewinsky, a former White House intern, who on tape admitted to gladly opening her mouth for the president, found herself in a room with intimidating FBI agents and assistant U.S. attorneys—just to make her admit that the president had lied about his sexual activities.

In Tsarist Russia the Inspector General controlled the Bureaucracy with his unspecified powers. Now the U.S. equivalent, the Independent Council, terrifies those who had any contact with Clinton by probing into every ooh and ah of the president's life—and that of the women with whom he says he had no sexual relationship.

In this new world order, scandal has replaced class struggle—at least in the media. Karl Marx couldn't have imagined that an assembly line worker, dizzy and tired after another speed up day at the global factory, would find distraction not in religion, the old opiate of the masses, but in speculating on the president's sex antics.

But it has little to do with working people's lives, or relationship with their families—unless of course a worker's daughter happened to take a White House tour one day and meet the president. Then she can expect a subpoena from Ken Starr and a grilling before a grand jury. Yes, welcome to the new world order. If history is truly finished, we now witness—thanks to the media, its favorite sinner, and the inspector general—the death of politics. The market wins another round. Long live shopping!

Smoke Gets in Your Whiskey Eyes

February 1, 1998

Americans have become zealous in their anti-tobacco crusade. Indeed, the California legislature went so far as to ban smoking in bars and clubs.

Now, the legislature is reconsidering—because many California bar patrons like to smoke while they drink, and because the powerful booze and bar owners lobby has exerted heavy pressure. I asked my friend, who regularly patronizes his local watering hole, what he thought about these recent developments.

"I never obeyed the darned law anyhow," he confessed. "I read about it in the papers, drove to my neighborhood bar, ordered a double bourbon with branch water and lit up. And no one said a word. The bartender winked at me. A dozen other people lit up and let me tell you we had a grand old time drinking bourbon and smoking cigarettes until the bar closed."

"Wait a second," I said. "You drove to the bar, drank and smoked all night. How exactly did you get home?"

"Why I hopped in my car and made it to my house in half the time it took me to get to the bar," he replied smugly.

"Don't you fear the consequences of driving after you've drunk that much?" I replied, making properly disapproving faces at him.

"I'm used to driving drunk," he replied. "Been doing it for years. I haven't hit a pedestrian yet, or even another car," he boasted.

"You know," I said, "you make a strong argument for allowing smoking in bars. How would you like to appear on my show? I'm in favor of banning smoking in bars, but I need a strong advocate on the other side. All you have to do is tell it like it is."

He smiled at me as he reached for a cigarette. "That's a nice offer. But the anti-smoking crusade has already offered me more money than you could afford to be a presenter at their big forum. You're too late."

"Darn," I said. "By the way, just in case I want to use a bar for a future show, what's the name of the one you patronize?"

"It's called Fools Rush In," he said. "And don't be afraid of second hand smoke. Its less dangerous than the crap they spray on your strawberries." He laughed.

I wondered, was he putting me on? Or is this whole debate about smoking in bars a put-on? A way to divert serious environmental thinking and action? Hmn!

Environmentalist Against Bombing Iraq

February 3, 1998

I'm an environmentalist—and darn proud of it. So, let me raise a question about the wisdom of bombing Saddam Hussein. Yes, he represents evil.

But remember the last war—or technological massacre! We turkey-shot the Iraqi army out of Kuwait. And it didn't cost us a dime, no small virtue in these budget-cutting days. And we took very few casualties from enemy fire.

But thousands of our troops suffer from Gulf War syndrome. The Pentagon hasn't revealed all it knows, but one theory attributes the sickness suffered by hundreds of Desert storm vets to ingesting poisons after our missiles hit chemical or biological weapons storage facilities. This unleashed a Pandora's Box of ills that disabled some and even led to birth defects.

Also, the Iraqis set fire to oil wells. The fire sent billowing clouds of carbon dioxide into the atmosphere. Not good for the lungs.

We destroyed Iraq's water treatment facilities. Not good for the environment or for Iraqis. Our media, however, hasn't yet discovered any other people living in Iraq besides Saddam and occasionally his foreign Minister, who always denies whatever our truth-printing media says.

Now, don't get me wrong, I want to see our armed forces punish Saddam Hussein for not letting our virtuous inspectors visit his palaces, where he probably stashes deadly chemical and biological weapons, but I'm worried.

Suppose we bomb a palace that houses Saddam Hussein's anthrax supply and our smart weapons hit the target and poof, the deadly toxin finds its way into the wind, which then blows over places where the good guys live—even here at home.

I'm no pacifist. But I don't want to see more burning oil wells. And I don't want to inhale an anthrax spore either. You might call me just a selfish environmentalist. But I think that's the best kind. No matter the polls say the American public wants President Clinton to bomb Saddam back into the Stone Age where he came from.

I believe in democracy and if the polls say bomb Saddam Hussein, who am I to go against the majority? In these days, a president that defies a poll is taking the first step on the road to monarchy or totalitarianism or whatever. I just say to my fellow Americans: don't rush to judgment before we know where all the anthrax is. We don't want more young Americans with Gulf War syndrome just because the bad guy didn't let our inspectors into the palace! Now that's my environmentalist argument against bombing Iraq.

Phooey on the Drug War

February 3, 1998

I'm sick and tired of the whole drug issue. Should we spend billions more on border patrols, military interdiction, police and prisons for drug users? Or should we educate and rehabilitate them? Should we increase penalties or decriminalize or actually legalize those substances that millions of Americans love to put into their noses, mouths or veins?

You know why I'm fed up with the discussion? I'll tell you. It's hypocrisy. Almost all Americans absorb large doses of addictive substances that are perfectly legal and often more dangerous than the illegal drugs.

How many of you can't start the day without a cup of coffee? How many still smoke? How many occasionally go on a toot or develop a mad craving that only a large Hershey bar can satisfy? How many can't sleep without pills, or stay awake without them?

A typical American drinks two cups of coffee before or with breakfast and continues drinking it throughout the day. He or she will smoke habitually or socially, and have a hit of chocolate five times a week. Millions survive on valium and Phenobarbital—legal opium. Others need speed, which they get from their doctors.

But those who smoke pot or do opium or snort coke or smoke crack—no worse than the legal prescriptions for health— are subject to long prison terms.

Of course, if you legalized drugs, what would happen to the millions around the world who work for police narcotic squads, or are prison guards or assistant district attorneys? What would happen to gun sales, to the drug cartel, to the economies of Bolivia, Peru and Colombia, where the coke is grown and processed? What would happen to Mexico and other places where economies depend on transshipment of illegal drugs? What would happen to the urine testing labs and the script writers who make their living from drug drama? And think of those who make their living from inventing slogans, like "Say No to Drugs." I know people who said no—but then did drugs anyway.

Would drugs become a total way of life in the poor neighborhoods and among certain groups of entertainers?

On second thought, let's go to a nearby bar and have a couple of drinks and maybe we can discuss drug policy in a rational way.

FDR's 1944 State of the Union

February 23, 1998

In 1944, 54 years ago, President Franklin Delano Roosevelt delivered his State of the Union address. In those days, I reminded my students, presidents delivered the address in March, not January.

"Who celebrates 54?" an aggressive student asked. "Twenty-five or 50—those are numbers the media associates with great events. Last year, for example, gun lovers celebrated the fiftieth birthday of the AK 47 rifle. Why 54?"

"Because," I said, "it's an excuse to have students review the text at a time when we witness politics undergoing the disease of banality, and the country experiencing a stress epidemic over fear of losing or not having jobs or health benefits."

In this speech, Roosevelt announced "a second Bill of Rights under which a new basis of security and prosperity can be established for all—regardless of station, race or creed."

He listed "The right to a useful and remunerative job. The right to earn enough to provide adequate food, clothing and recreation."

"Compare that," I said, "to Alan Greenspan's need to maintain a healthy rate of unemployment, or to Clinton's assault on welfare recipients."

" 'The right of every family to a decent home,' " I continued quoting Roosevelt, because " 'necessitous men are not freemen.' "

"Do you know of plans to house the millions of homeless, to prevent evictions of those who lose their jobs?" I asked.

"The right to adequate medical care," Roosevelt continued, "the right to adequate protection from the economic fears—old age, sickness, accident and unemployment. The right to a good education."

"True individual freedom cannot exist without economic security," FDR said.

The class was quiet.

Clinton promotes agri-business and banking interests. Roosevelt talked about the "right of every farmer to raise and sell his own products at a return which will give him and his family a decent living."

"The few small farmers left would laugh bitterly," I said.

"The right of every businessman," Roosevelt continued, "to trade in an atmosphere of freedom from unfair competition and domination by monopolies at home and abroad."

"In the NAFTA-GATT era, governments serve monopolies at home and abroad and thus unfair competition," I reminded the class.

Roosevelt concludes that "All of these rights spell security. And after this war is over we must be prepared to move forward, in the implementation of these rights, to new goals of human happiness and well being."

"Well," I said, "what do you think?"

"Those old fashioned goals don't fit our era," said one woman. "Freedom now means extending the death penalty to underage people and the right to shop, 24 hours a day, in person or over the phone.

"How about the unemployed, homeless, hungry without access to medical care?" I asked.

"Hey professor," another said, "the empathy tank is empty!"

"Well, refill it," I said. "It costs nothing to expand your intellect or your feelings for less fortunate people."

Thanks, FDR.

Hot Lots for Sale at Nevada Test Site

March 3, 1998

You know how government officials use benign euphemisms to conceal deadly truths? Did you hear about the "stockpile stewardship program"? The friendly stewards work at the Nevada test site to redesign nuclear testing. After the 1992 international moratorium on atomic tests, national security workers started to worry about their jobs.

According to the February 14 *Economist* magazine, the government needed 11,000 workers to detonate those "devices", as the nuclear gang called their pet bombs. The government even filmed the tests. You see the explosion, hear the boom, and then see a mushroom cloud appears. Cut to the fire storm bending mighty trees and setting buildings aflame with mannequins inside. Someone built those mock houses and made sure that no despondent Las Vegas losers wandered into the test area.

Well, the post-Cold War era called for the downsizing of 8,000 of those loyal workers, but left 3,000 to continue the program. Now, they will conduct "subcritical tests" to determine the health of our nuclear arsenal.

No, they're not taking blood from plutonium triggers or measuring the temperature of hydrogen bombs. But they are—in violation of the test ban agreements—making sure that the 20 thousand plus nuclear weapons don't have blown fuses or loose screws.

What's more important, abiding by a test ban treaty or re-welding possible stress points on our ICBMs? Hey, national security demands nothing less! But the Energy Department, in the spirit of the 1990s, intends to privatize the test site area. Yes, with the Cold War over, they can "market" the public's land. Visualize the Secretary of Energy wearing a Groucho Marx mustache selling real estate. "These lots are not only big, but they're very deep."

Well, the desert around the nuclear test site is also very hot—and not only from the sun. Since the early 1950s, the sand has sucked up radioactive particles from over 1000 nuclear explosions.

You can start a solar-energy plant, launch communications satellites or build a trailer park for downsized test site workers! Construct a new mall on top of the alpha-beta-gamma particles! Surely, you'll believe the Department of Energy when it tells you that the low level radiation that clings to the ground can't hurt you. They've told that one to lots of people who accidentally absorbed radiation from the tests. Some got cancer and died. Big deal, that wasn't the only factor that could have caused tumors to grow.

So, if you're looking for a bargain and you believe the government's line about low level radiation being no more dangerous than drinking tap water—hmn?—well, go for it. There's gold in that there desert—even if it is a bit radioactive.

Praise the Lord
and Pass the Olestra Chips

March 12, 1998

Proctor and Gamble makes lots of items you buy in the supermarket—from laundry soaps to wholesome snacks. But proponents of healthy diet claimed that P&G soaked their snack food with concentrated fats, salt and chemicals—bad for your health.

Well, as we know, science solves all problems. So, P&G directed its chemists to develop a fat substitute, a substance that provides that compelling fried and greasy taste, but without adding a spare tire to your waistline, clogging your arteries or causing you severe indigestion.

After 30 years of frustrating experiments that cost P&G some $500 million, the geniuses emerged from the labs with a product called Olestra, a finger-licking-good fat substitute that was free from the dreaded curse of calories.

The FDA approved the product. P&G licensed Olestra to the Frito-Lay company, which began to market non-fat Pringle chips. For two years, promoters handed out free samples to chip-loving passersby on streets throughout the Midwest.

A few people later reported that they suffered stomach cramping and diarrhea, but most recipients of the free samples said, "Yum yum." Some troublemakers have tried to scare patriotic Olestra-eating Americans with the idea that the product could cause intestinal damage. These mischief makers have even demanded that the California Attorney General determine whether commercials made for this tasty chemical should contain the warning: "Olestra may cause cramping and loose stools."

This is obscene. It's fortunate that most Americans don't know the euphemism "stool."

But they know all the nuances related to obesity and heart attacks. Poor P&G, who thought they had the perfect answer. Olestra tastes like real fat but eludes the calorie-cholesterol trap.

The bio-engineers did it: a substance that the body can't digest—like grass or tree bark. But it does give you fiber.

Some irresponsible media types have seized on the supposed gastrointestinal effects of eating Olestra-soaked chips, even claiming it produced "fecal urgency" or "anal leakage."

Overly-cautious scientists warned that Olestra can inhibit the absorption of vitamin C and two Harvard nutritionists, Doctors Willett and Stampfer, wrote that there is "strong reason to suspect that the effects (of Olestra) will include increases in cancer, heart diseases, stroke, and blindness."

Well, what would you choose—a potato chip fried in grease that could clog your arteries, or an equally delicious morsel that doesn't add to your waistline or cholesterol count? I'm going to eat one right now. Crunch, crunch. Umh. You'd never know that it doesn't contain real grease.

I've swallowed it and there are no side effects. So, let me conclude that science can solve problems in the end. I stand in witness that Olestra tastes good and has no unpleasant side effects…Oops, I urgently have to see a man about a horse. Bye.

Privatize Spying?

April 7, 1998

Good grief, yet another CIA "secrets" scandal! Douglas Groat, "a disgruntled member of the CIA unit that breaks into foreign embassies to steal code books," tried to extort money from the CIA, for not telling their secrets. The CIA fired Groat in 1996. He then apparently alerted the victim countries about CIA break-ins. Is there no end to the leakage of vital secrets to our mortal enemies? I felt vulnerable, so I called on my CIA contact, Smiley C. George, for reassurance.

"Mr. Groat supposedly broke into foreign embassies to steal their secret communication codes," I said. "Isn't that a crime, something the CIA isn't supposed to do?"

"What are you, some naive liberal? The CIA is supposed to do all in its power for U.S. security. Without a viable enemy in the world, this pretense becomes more difficult to sustain and you end up with a frustrated character like Groat, who feels unappreciated and tries to get his feelings compensated through money."

"What has caused this flood of infidelity to our country?" I asked.

"The market," he replied. "Everything else is up for sale, why not secrets? In the 1980s and 90s, Aldrich Ames and Harold Nicholson made money peddling worthless CIA files to the Soviets and then foolishly got caught. My God, these guys practically wore sandwich board signs, saying, 'Get your red hot secrets here.' "

"Slow down," I said. "Are you saying that the CIA has no vital secrets—that what was sold during the Cold War to the dreaded Soviets didn't matter?"

"Ask yourself: what did Moscow do with the piles of information Ames and Nicholson sold them? The Russkies threw in the towel, that's what they did, and we won the Cold War. Maybe the secrets told them how truly weak they were and how strong we were. Ames should get a medal, not a prison sentence."

"I don't get it," I confessed. "Didn't Ames give truly vital information to our enemy?"

"Like what?" he asked

"Well," I stuttered, "I don't know. The material is classified."

"How come the Soviets, our declared enemy, knew our secrets and never told anyone about them? And, moreover, if the Russians knew them, why can't you or any other citizen know them?"

"Wow," I said, "I never thought about that. How should we deal with our secrets?"

"Privatize them," he said. "Get with the times—there's a great market out there for secrets. We could take bids on them, like defense contractors, as to who could most profitably sell our secrets. Foreign governments or private spy companies would buy them and maybe resell them. The private sector would prosper. The government could tax profits on secrets."

"But national secrets, that's our security."

"Hey," he said, "we're talking about privatizing social security. Why not national security?"

Don't Get Stiffed by the Drug Companies

May 4, 1998

Some big, strong men have what Archie Bunker once referred to as connubial problems. But Pfizer drug company now has the answer.

This miracle drug apparently has side effects: you better take it with eight ounces of water—if it gets stuck in your throat you get a stiff neck.

Seriously, some guys' marriages crumble because they became sexually challenged, so to speak. Inability to perform can lead to family breakdown, nervous anxiety, depression—even suicide. But other guys feel compelled to perform morning, noon and night. With Viagra in the pharmacies, they tell their doctors that they suffer from impotence and they get a prescription. Men apparently will risk possible long-term harm from yet unknown side effects just for the possibility of having more sex.

Impotence results from our civilization, some of the great psychiatrists believed. Since God is credited with the superior attributes, people are left with lesser virtues and possibilities. Religion punished people for original sin. The internal projection of this sin, which translates as sensuality, often results in impotence. And impotence can make life desolate—just ask the people who suffer from it.

Now a drug that will cure all that?

Hmn! Remember D. H. Lawrence made Lady Chatterly's husband impotent as a result of a war wound. The husband in the novel represents the impotence of the British upper class. The non-frigid women, like Lady Chatterly, sought partners more active, shall we say, than her husband. The working class gardener did not need Viagra, as you will recall.

But Viagra is being marketed to women as well.

The drug, according to scientists, probably can cause blood to rush to the area often referred to as the source of sexual dysfunction. But lack of desire stems from deeper themes—often the character of the men in a woman's life and the artificial stimulation of the physiological factors cannot reach the source of the so-called frigid woman's discontent.

A retired friend of man asked me whether Viagra could work for older men and women as well

"I don't know," I told him, "but it's clear that lots of men see sex the way they see life: keeping score. That doesn't disappear when men get older."

There's the story of the 95-year-old Mafia don who tells his doctor he needs help because his 95-year-old cousin, also a Mafioso, says he has sex twice daily with a teenaged girl.

"Help me, Doc," the Mafioso said. "What can I do?"

"You could say the same thing," the doctor said.

I think I better not say anything else.

What Do You Tell the Kids?

January, 28 1998

I've tried unsuccessfully to get my kid, now eleven, to read something besides the comics in the newspaper. Thanks to the sensationalized media and with assists from Bill Clinton, Paula Jones and Monica Lewinsky, my kid now reads headlines and even lead stories.

This puts parents into a pickle. What do you say when the kid says: "Dad, I'm reading the newspaper, like you wanted and I have questions: What's oral sex? Is it the same as kissing?"

Hardly pausing, I countered: "Why aren't you reading about Netanyahu and Arafat? The important story is about the Middle East and a possible breakthrough on Israeli withdrawal from the West Bank."

My eleven-year-old made a sour face. "Are they having an affair? Dad, what does it mean that Monica Lewinsky wanted to earn her presidential kneepads?"

"Maybe the White House has organized a hockey game for interns," I said. "But why aren't you interested in the Pope's visit to Cuba? That's important because it might lead to the lifting of the U.S. embargo. If you watched the news and the McNeill-Lehrer show or whatever they call it now, you would have deeper knowledge of the world."

She yawned.

"Daddy, did Clinton have sex with other women? Is that what he did that was bad? Or was it not telling Hillary? Did Hillary forgive him and give him another chance? Did Hillary have oral sex? Is she a lesbian? Mrs. Carradine down the block has sex with the gardener. If she was president would that become news?"

I felt overwhelmed "Look," I said, "this is very delicate."

"You mean what the president did, or your inability to come out and tell me that Monica Lewinsky bent down and—"

"Stop," I shouted. "How come you asked if you already knew?"

"Dad, I watch *Melrose Place* and *Beverly Hill 90210* and those shows are tame compared to the TV and newspaper headlines over the last week. I think I'll stop watching them and see more news shows because they're more interesting. I saw a one-hour special on Monica that replaced *Home Improvement*. It's great to hear grownups discuss sex on TV with the parents not throwing the censor switch."

I was speechless. I drove her to school. I turned on Rush Limbaugh, who was having audio orgasms over Clinton's plight and he announced that a newspaper had taken a poll of Washington women, asking would they sleep with Bill Clinton. seventy percent answered "Never Again." My daughter laughed.

"Did you understand that?" I asked.

"Yes, Dad, it was a joke. But you have to admit that Bill Clinton has made learning about the birds and bees a lot more fun."

The CIA Is "Ageist"

May 8, 1998

An enticing ad appeared in last Sunday's *New York Times* (May 4, 1989), Central Intelligence Agency offers "The Ultimate International experience."

"Wow," I said to myself. "I might be qualified." I read further.

"For the extraordinary individual who wants more than a job…a way of life that will challenge the deepest resources of your intelligence, self reliance, and responsibility. It demands an adventurous spirit…a forceful personality…superior intellectual ability…toughness of mind…and the highest degree of integrity.

"This is the Clandestine Service, the vital element of intelligence collection…the cutting edge of American intelligence, an elite corps gathering the vital information needed by our policymakers to make critical decisions."

I had fantasies.

I imagined myself on the streets of Teheran, in 1953, disguised as a Mullah, shooting a supporter of Premier Mossadegh. "Take that," I said, "for our oil interests."

In Guatemala in 1954, I chased into exile those pseudo reds who backed democratically elected President Arbenz. "Viva United Fruit Company," I shouted.

I daydreamed that I passed guns to assassins of Lumumba in Africa in 1960. "Long Live Union Miniere—the Belgian mining company."

I landed on the beach at the Bay of Pigs. I didn't dwell on that one.

Images came faster: annihilating a village in Vietnam; bombing Cambodia. "That'll make 'em see light at the end of the tunnel," McNamara told me.

Nixon, Kissinger and the president of IT&T thanked me for destabilizing Chile. Jesse Helms patted me on the back for delivering land mines to Savimbi in Angola. Bill Casey thanked me for providing surface-to-air missiles to fanatic Muslim Afghani freedom fighters and assigned me to work with Ollie North to get arms to the Nicaraguan Contras. Corpses flooded my consciousness.

I changed gears and imagined myself sipping a dry martini, shaken not stirred, while some gorgeous woman moaned amidst the rumpled counterpane. I fired exotic weapons, escaped enemy agents in tropical jungles. "I'm tripping," I told myself.

To bring myself back to reality, I called a guy I know at the CIA and asked him who wrote this copy.

"Some kid in an ad agency," he said.

"I guess the guys who gave the presidents decades of worthless information on the Soviet Union's growing power while the Soviet system was collapsing must have retired. Maybe this is a new CIA," I said.

"Nope," he said. "Same old, same old. Were you thinking of applying?"

"Yes," I said. "I need some excitement."

"Well, try bungie jumping," he said. "Read further in the ad: 'Maximum age for entrance into this program is 35.'"

"Damn," I said. "That's the last straw. The CIA is, is, is..." I said, searching for the right word to describe this agency that has assassinated, overthrown governments, made millions into refugees, "it's, it's ageist."

Selling Weapons and Democracy

June 2, 1998

Defense Secretary William Cohen returned from Latin American in late May. Cynics suspected he was selling sophisticated U.S. weapons to those emerging democracies. You see, Latin America is now democratic, except for Cuba, of course.

Of the five days in Argentina, Chile and Brazil, Cohen says he did not market U.S. weapons, but preached greater civilian control over the military. In many of these nations, the military still operates with minimum civilian control. In Chile, for example, General Pinochet, bless his soul, enacted a law that allocates 10 percent of the country's annual copper exports to the armed forces for weapons purchases.

Cohen told *Miami Herald* reporter Andres Oppenheimer that "we don't seek to impose any system on any country, but I believe civilian control is a key element of a modern democracy. Civilian control over the military insures accountability to the electorate, rather than to a designated elite.'"

By elite, Cohen meant former generals who are now defense ministers and have virtual monopolies over weapons acquisitions.

"Why does the United States want civilians in charge of Latin American militaries?" I asked an honest Pentagon official, who decided it would not help his career to be identified.

"Frankly, it makes it easier to sell them expensive weapons. Members of Congress could ask why we sell F-16s or Bradley fighting vehicles to guys accused of mass murder by human rights groups. And just to cover our butt, we're opening a new center in Washington to study defense. We've recently funded the National Defense University, which created the Center of Hemispheric Defense Studies to train Latin American civilians on military issues."

"Train them in what?"

"To keep weapons sales going indefinitely," he said.

"Is there no real defense need involved in these sales?"

"Of course there's need. How else could weapons manufacturers sell modern arms to say Chile, Venezuela or Uruguay?
See, when one country buys a new jet fighter, the others have to
buy the equivalent fighter. Then all these countries have our arms
and the Pentagon goes to Congress and says: 'Look those countries have weapons as advanced as ours. We need new and more
expensive ones.' "

"But is there no aspect of defense involved?"

"Of course there is! Suppose uppity populations rebel.
Modern jet fighters intimidate even the toughest civilians.
Remember during the 1973 coup in Chile, how those Hawker
Hunter missiles zipped right through the windows of Allende's
presidential Palace in Chile? Heh Heh!

"The next time people take this democracy talk too seriously and start to assert popular control these weapons will be a
great defense."

"Against whom? What?"

"The people," he snapped. "Democracy. What else are these
weapons supposed to fight in Latin America?"

Educating Crows

July 22, 1998

A Spanish saying warns that if you educate crows, they will pluck out your eyes. In 1960, the CIA educated thousands of Cuban exile crows to invade Cuba. The CIA also created a special corps of super-vicious crows, like Hitler's Waffen SS, to mop up the Castroites after the invasion succeeded.

But after the April 1961 Bay of Pigs invasion failed, the Agency continued its education of a crow named Luis Posada Carriles. They taught him intelligence and guerrilla warfare methods—along with Felix Rodriguez and Jorge Mas Canosa. Rogriguez later became a well known CIA official who supervised Che Guevara's 1967 assassination in Bolivia.

Posada joined Venezuelan intelligence. Mas went into business and in 1980, founded and then headed, until his death from cancer last year, the Cuban American National Foundation, CANF.

Under Mas, CANF established itself as a respectable, anti-Castro organization that controlled major aspects of U.S.-Cuba policy—until recent events destroyed the non-violent facade. Even before Posada dropped his information bomb on the *New York Times* on July 12th and 13th, U.S. Customs agents in October, 1997, had detained four anti-Castro Cubans off the Puerto Rico shore. The men had sniper rifles on their small boat. "They're to assassinate Castro," one of the arrested boasted. U.S. officials traced the ownership of the rifles and the boat to leaders of CANF.

Posada admitted that Mas and other CANF heavies had financed Posada's assassination plots, while the FBI and CIA winked.

Mas Canosa, like Posada, was a hard-core crow. Posada plotted the bombings. Mas paid for them. "Whenever I needed money," Posada said, "he (Mas) said to give me $5,000, give me $10,000, give me $15,000, and they (CANF) sent it to me." He received more than $200,000 over the years for terrorism.

The very U.S. national security agencies who have for decades labeled Cuba as a terrorist state were waging their terrorist war against Cuba.

Did U.S. officials know of Posada's activities surrounding the bombing of a civilian Cubana airliner over Barbados? Seventy-three people died. Venezuela then arrested Posada, but he miraculously escaped prison in the mid-1980s. Lt. Col. Oliver North eagerly hired him in El Salvador to supply the Nicaraguan contras. North's notes, subpoenaed by Congress during the Iran-Contras hearings, indicate that Mas Canosa paid a $50,000 bribe to Venezuelan prison guards to abet Posada's jail break.

Posada also worked with Antonio Veciana, who told me last year that in 1975 the CIA paid him $250,000 for his decade-long attempt to assassinate Fidel Castro. Veciana said he teamed up with Posada in 1972 to mount a gun inside a TV camera. Posada hired hitmen to pose as a Venezuelan TV crew to cover Fidel Castro's visit to Chile. The killers chickened out when they realized they had no escape route. Curses, foiled again!

Last year, Posada boasted of plotting a series of bombings of Cuban tourist installations. An Italian tourist died in one of them. "It is sad that someone is dead," he said. "The Italian was sitting in the wrong place at the wrong time." Posada labeled the bombings acts of war intended to cripple Cuba's economy by scaring off tourism and investment. Yet, Italy is our NATO partner, not part of the commie conspiracy. The dead Italian's family must be wondering about the thoughts of an educated crow. Did his trainers learn anything? Why do I even ask?

The Pollution Honor System

August 23, 1995

The Mexican equivalent of our EPA made a shocking announcement on August 21st. Mexican officials discovered that 62 percent of factories inspected were violating environmental laws. That means some 5000 out of 7781 factories failed to comply with environmental law.

Ford Motor Company and Volkswagen rank among the 5000. In light of all the assurances that U.S. and Mexican leaders gave us when they were promoting NAFTA, what can this alarming development mean for life on both sides of the border?

But not to worry just because there's no mechanism to force these polluters to comply with minimum standards, the companies will police themselves! It's part of the overall global campaign to trust business and privatize everything.

Twenty-two companies have already signed agreements with the Mexican Office of the Environment. They've graciously agreed to monitor their own environmental impact and to improve pollution control. Indeed, the CEOs of these companies have committed over $13 million over the next two years to clean up the messes they've made. Both Ford and VW signed this self-auditing agreement. One Mexican CEO hailed the honor system as a bridge-building step of trust between industry and government.

Instead of fining these contaminators for dumping their PCBs in the river and their ozone-depleting gases into the air, Mexican authorities smiled with satisfaction over what one called "the best solution we have for cleaning up the environment without ruining the country's industrial productivity."

My friend Nacho teaches ecology at a Mexican university. I asked him what he thought about the accord. "Would you trust the fox to inspect the hen house?" he asked. "Well, that's what this agreement means. The government says that the best way to have a safe environment is to trust the corporate leaders who are destroying the environment to suddenly become model citizens."

"And you don't think these very wealthy and important people will be responsible?" I asked.

"Would you trust Jesse James to inspect the bank vault?"

"You mean that all the promises made about NAFTA making our environment safer weren't true?"

"You mean you actually believed Henry Kissinger's promises?" Nacho looked at me. "I can offer you the deal of a lifetime. How'd you like to buy the Brooklyn Bridge for only $10?" he asked.

But all the corporate leaders can't be as cynical as Nacho said. They too have to live with the pollution in the air, soil and water.

"Yes," Nacho agreed. "But they buy purified water, have air filtering systems in their homes and offices and buy only organically-grown food."

"So, what's the solution?"

Nacho took a hit off his oxygen tank, put on his face mask and prepared to go into the street. "I personally believe in long prison sentences for environmental criminals."

IMF Blames Mexicans

August 30, 1995

Do you remember how foreign investors supposedly panicked at the end of 1994 and took their money out of Mexico when the government devalued the peso? Then good President Clinton and noble Secretary of the Treasury Robert Rubin rescued poor Mexico by pouring billions of our dollars in—but only as loans, of course.

Well, an IMF report suggests that Mexican speculators, not gringos, sent their money across the Rio Grande to safety. That's what freedom means, or free market economy, whatever. Their money fled, they didn't, because we don't let them in; their money is of course welcome.

Anyway, the IMF discovered that some lucky Mexican billionaires had an educated hunch that their government was going to devalue the peso. Gee, who could have told them?

In November and December 1994, just before devaluation, Mexican reserves fell by $9 billion. Yet, during that same period, foreign investors sold only $370 million of their Mexican paper and made new purchases for almost the same amount. Some of the drop reflects the Mexican trade imbalance, but the IMF sleuths deduced that the real culprits, the Mexican high rollers, knew devaluation was coming and didn't want to see their fortunes reduced by 50 percent.

What lessons can we learn from this? The Mexican government lied to its people about the true state of its economy, while insiders leaked word or sold information about the impending devaluation to well-connected friends. The high rolling Mexicans who had pledged their eternal loyalty to their patria did remain in Mexico. They only sent their money abroad—for better treatment.

Another lesson, anyone who wants to get rich quickly on the backs of poor, third world people faces the prospect that the host government could devalue the currency.

Wall Street's lesson? If a country does devaluate, the U.S. government will rescue the investors—because the worst thing that could happen in capitalism is that rich gamblers should suffer because they took a risk.

The rich Mexicans rescued their dough, Clinton saved the American investors! So what's the big deal? The IMF phumphets about the Mexican government's lying. Next they'll discover that the pope's a Catholic.

The poor and middle class now work twice the hours to receive the same pay as nine months ago. Mexican patriots who saved their money in Mexican banks had their savings cut in half.

Well, that's real capitalism for you. In the text book it says that by working hard and saving money you'll prosper. One editor has removed the qualifying phrase: if you're from a wealthy family.

For those politically correct investors who don't like places that rip off their people, think of Henny Youngman's friend who got his nose broken in two places. Now he stays out of those places.

Safeguard

October 25, 1995

Move over, Statue of Liberty. Make way for Operation Safeguard. The tired and huddled masses have gone the way of the five-cent cigar. Welcome to the global village! Welcome free traders, free investors, but free migration? Forget it. It's us against them.

Last year, to protect Arizona citizens from a deluge of Mexicans, super migra cops detained and returned some 230,000 undocumented Mexicans. In Texas and California they sent another quarter of a million packing. The INS doesn't mention how many Mexicans evaded scrutiny and today care for our kids, pick our food, cook our meals and clean our homes and offices.

But, anyway, congratulations, Operation Safeguard members! Your capture figures alone justified your increased budget, which bought 75 new patrols, two fingerprint scanning computers, two helicopters, five video cameras, hundreds of binoculars and a partridge in a pear tree.

A border patrolman told me he took no satisfaction in rounding up poor Mexicans and sending them back across the border. "It's pushing rocks up mountains," he said. "Last year we deported 39 percent more undocumented than the year before. This year we expect even more because of Mexico's economic collapse. A lot of them don't speak English or Spanish. They're Indians who can't make it anywhere in Mexico. I feel for them but what the hell, we can't afford to have them here. But there's a bright side."

I waited with bated breath for the good news.

"We're probably going to get much more money to build sensor posts along the border and new weapons that will allow for even heavier measures."

"You mean more technology and increased use of violence, will help you keep the undocumented people out?"

"No," he said, "it means more new jobs here."

"Aha. Do you enjoy your job?" I asked.

"I protect you and other citizens from a tidal wave of poor foreigners, not all of them the most desirable of people. How'd you like to be living next to some five foot tall Indian who doesn't speak any language you know, can't read or write, but makes a lotta babies? I do my duty, sir. Until the Mexican government decides to police its own frontier, the job falls on us."

I almost saluted. Is there a humane way out? More loans to President Zedillo while we wait for neo-liberalism to work its miracle cures? Mexico is our neighbor. Our free trade partner. Twenty-five million Mexican Americans live in this country. We never promised them free passage of people, just goods and money. Operation Safeguard, *sí*, Statue of Liberty, *no*. Welcome to the mid 90s.

A Guide to Mexican Reality

November 7-8, 1995

Do you know where Reality is and how to get there? Fly to Tuxtla Gutierrez, capital of Chiapas, take a *colectivo* to San Cristobal de las Casas, an old colonial city an hour and a half and two mountains away. Go see the person who communicates with the Zapatistas and find out when and where your appointment is.

Early Sunday evening the contact informs me that my filming date was two hours ago, but not to worry because if I arrive there tomorrow morning they will understand. Miraculously, Rebecca, my partner, and I find Carlos Martinez, a cameraman with a camera, charged batteries and tape, and I locate an open rental agency that has a front wheel drive VW Combi. At 11:30 we put our heads on pillows.

At 4 AM Monday morning we depart, south to Comitan, about an hour and a half drive on a pothole-filled, but nevertheless paved road. Head east 20 more miles to Las Margaritas and then continue on a rocky, unpaved road that begins to resemble a mountain trail.

Enjoy magnificent scenery, occasional Indian villages and periodic threats to your life as the vehicle skids down slippery mud slopes with nothing but 200 feet of space between you and the bottom of the canyon. On these steep roads local people tote what look like 100-pound loads of firewood on their backs.

After about three hours of robust kidney exercise you arrive at the village of Guadalupe Tepeyac, a ghost town, the residents driven out by the Federales, the Mexican army, an occupation force. In the village, doctors and nurses sit outside a modern hospital bereft of patients. Armed soldiers amble along the muddy lanes between abandoned houses and a few hookers sit on a rickety bench, waiting for the soldiers to finish their shift.

On the way out of the village, we pass a military camp. A soldier stands in the entrance—a makeshift bamboo gate—snapping a photo of the side of the vehicle as it drives by. Ah, modern security procedures!

We continue east for another half an hour, sliding, literally, down the slippery slopes into Reality. In Spanish, Reality is La Realidad, the name of this village in the Lacondon jungle, in southeast Chiapas, maybe fifteen miles north of the Guatemalan border, midway between Las Margaritas on the West and San Quintin on the East.

Yes, a wooden sign assures you, this is La Realidad, Reality. Park your vehicle on the side of the road, says a short, dark-skinned man who approaches and asks you in non-syntactical Spanish to write down what you want and give him some ID. He turns out to be the elected village chief. Villagers call him Maxi, which I assume to be short for *maximum jefe*, but is actually an abbreviation for his name, Maximiliano.

I write I had a date with *"el sup,"* Subcomandante Marcos. He asks me if I had brought the newspapers or anything else. We had departed before the morning papers arrived, so I gave him a book and some cigars for Comandante Moises, a gift from a friend of his in the city.

He nods, and tells us to park the vehicle in a smidgen of shade offered by a tree near the village classroom, next to the stream that runs through the village.

We wait throughout the morning as colorfully clad, bare-footed women and teenage girls return from the mountains carrying formidable loads of wood on their backs with a sling-like affair that reaches around the wood and across their foreheads to absorb and balance the weight. We watched from a crude bench outside the two-room school. Sounds came from the children and teachers inside. The air hangs around us like a cartoon bubble that says "heat and humidity," as the foggy cool of early morning turns furnace-like once the sun burns away the mist. At 11:00 A.M., a dozen lower-grade school school-boys run out of the classrooms, doing somersaults.

Surrounding us, rising precipitously from the valley, green mountains stand like still-life paintings; tropical Vermeers, studded with fir trees, precious wood, banana stalks and, hiding under them, the frail coffee trees—key to the village economy.

The village itself should have posed for a picture postcard. From above one sees a well-ordered pattern of thatched huts, divided by a rapidly-running mountain stream, with women and girls washing corn, beans, clothes and bodies and little kids splashing and frolicking. Firewood is piled neatly in sheds outside the huts and wisps of smoke curl from the kitchens. (Later, we learn that smoke protects villagers from the insect perils of the area). Dogs yap and roosters crow amidst a continual croaking and humming of frogs and bugs, with pigs snorting like bass players in this tropical orchestra of fauna.

Noontime comes and goes and still no word from "*el sup*." Maybe he's in the middle of writing one of his communiqués for the internet or meeting with the other comandantes about political strategy, or reading yesterday's *La Jornada* or this week's *Proceso*, Mexico's best and most progressive newspaper and magazine respectively. Maybe he's in the middle of a hot poker game or hunting an animal or making love to his wife, girlfriend, boyfriend or whomever. Am I feeling a bit frustrated?

The dense humidity begins to hang from everything, especially my clothes and hair. I slug my bottled water both to quench my thirst and temper my hunger pangs. Out of nowhere a buzzing black insect, an image from a gameboy set, circles my head. I wait. It lands on my hand. I slap. Got it! Within seconds a large red spot appears with a black dot in the center. It itches. I resist scratching. It starts to burn. Yeah, I got it all right.

At about three P.M., village men return from the *milpa*, the corn patch. Banal hunger pangs now intrude on any lofty thoughts and feelings I might have. Carlos arranges with the village head to allow us to buy our meals at the house of Jorge's family—for ten pesos a meal, about $1.15. By four, we begin to think "*el sup*" has forgotten us, or the message didn't arrive or he's at an all day prayer meeting.

To hell with him, I say, let's eat.

We wander across the so-called road to Jorge's house. His wife, Gloria, and his kids laugh as we arrive, place hunks of log or kiddie chairs outside the kitchen, plus a small bench, on which a teenage girl, dressed in what looks like her party clothes but which turns out to be traditional women's costume, places a metal bowl of water—for us to wash our hands. She smiles as we fumble with the bowl and try to figure out where to wipe our wet hands. Her jet black hair is perfectly combed, adorned with a bow. She is seventeen, unmarried, one of Jorge and Gloria's eight children. Two others died shortly after birth.

Gloria has cooked us a veritable feast, tepid, flaky corn tortillas, and watery, over-salted beans with pieces of protein—insects and worms—floating in them. She brings a dish with salt, limes and tiny chili peppers. I stuff some beans in my tortilla, jam two tiny peppers in and take a bite. The hair on my ears liquefies, a dentist drills into a nerve on the roof of my mouth.

"We call them look-at-the-sky peppers," says the teenager. As my body temperature reestablishes its equilibrium a small puppy approaches, an animal slightly larger than a mouse, with the pathetic look of a beagle mixed with a tortured rabbit. "She has no name," responds Gloria. I name her *Giganta*, giant, the Saint Bernard of the Lacondon Jungle.

After dinner, about 4:30, I wander over to the village basketball court—every village has one—and the guys invite me to play with them. I have never before, at 5'7" and 155 pounds, been the tallest and heaviest player on the court. The net-less hoops, one of which hangs at a 45 degree angle, present a challenge. A village ref whistles the violations and we change sides after our team scores 20 points.

Our side wins, but I decline my right as member of the winning team to play in a second game and slosh my way off the court. My bloated feet, clad in hiking boots, throb explosively, my clothes cling like freshly glued wallpaper.

Then comes night, the young men still shooting hoops by the full moon, as a chill fills the air, chasing away all but the most determined of people-chewing insects. Wearing sweat pants, sweat shirt and a pair of cotton socks midway up my legs, drenching myself with insect repellent, I curl up in the rear bench of the VW Combi, Rebecca on the middle bench, leaving only a crack of window open—a mistake, as I discover the next morning.

Carlos, the jungle veteran, drapes his hammock with mosquito netting inside the classroom. Roosters crow, frogs and insects chatter away, an occasional whinny comes from a horse, a snort from a pig—Reality's nighttime band.

At about 3:30 Tuesday morning, I awake and notice that some women have begun their trek up the mountainside; others are washing baskets of grain in the nearby stream. I stare at the sky for a couple of hours, then at 5:30 put my boots over the throbbing, itching welts on my ankles and legs and limp toward the communal water tap to throw something cold and wet on my face.

The men begin to file toward the *milpa*, machetes well-filed, faces stoic. Like the women who awoke before them and began their labors two hours earlier, the village men have followed a work-life pattern for centuries. They have relocated when the conquistadors and their descendants drove them into the jungle and obliged them to incorporate Catholicism into their own, far broader and more complex world view.

In La Realidad, some, mostly women, still speak in Tojolabal. The majority speak "Castilla," but haltingly, without evidence of developed vocabularies or syntax. They know what they have learned, however, from their parents, grandparents, and great-grandparents: a culture of order, discipline, respect for Nature and each other—and a democratic, albeit hierarchical, system of government, where the village meets in Assembly to discuss each important decision. Then, a pseudo-military command structure carries out the decisions.

This village is 100 percent Zapatista. In October, elected delegates of Mexico's Congress, along with Bishop Samuel Ruiz and other dignitaries, met here with Zapatista leaders. Many residents of La Realidad prepared for the meetings by slipping bandannas over their mouths and noses and hoisting sticks onto their shoulders, simulating rifles—the Zapatista symbol. The mask identifies the Mayan as a member of the EZLN. He or she takes off the bandanna or ski mask to hide—just another villager who fetches wood, washes corn and hacks the weeds from the *milpa*.

Driven to the inhospitable terrain by progress, cattle ranchers, timber barons and coffee estate owners, by hydroelectric projects and oil drilling, by corrupt and venal political bosses who fostered division inside the Indian communities, by the laws of capital as they have operated for five centuries, these people now face the ultimate threat of annihilation thanks to NAFTA— a subject I was eager to discuss with "*el sup*", if he ever showed up.

I wander with the crew over to Jorge's kitchen where the fire is well stoked, the beans are bubbling, and I pray the coffee water was boiled. Same people, same logs, same pathetic dog, same meal—except this time there's a burned egg thrown on top of the beans, and the chilis are green, not red and burn the roof of my mouth only 85 percent as much as the scarlet killers did.

After breakfast I send another note to "*el sup*"—short of begging, just a polite reminder that we're waiting. We watch the thin, white cover of mist burn away and the jungle sun hurling its daily challenge at the human body.

Antonio, another visitor in waiting, shows us where we can dip our itching, throbbing, sweating bodies into the cool stream. We trudge a quarter of a mile on a mud path and immerse hot flesh in cool mountain water. It is 11 am. Women begin to descend from the mountain with their wood piles. We watch grass, insects, and kids running out of school, trying to figure out who these weirdoes are.

The school teachers chat with us. One of the two young women from Mexico City says that the rebellion of January 1, 1994 gave meaning to her life; the ability to serve in areas that desperately needed teachers. The volunteer nurses had similar explanations. They give Rebecca a list of medicines they need for TB, fungus infections and other common ailments that make villagers miserable—or kill them.

The people of La Realidad suffer a high infant mortality rate, low life expectancy and terrible illnesses while they live. A granny with a kid slung across her back and another in tow told me her daughter-in-law had died and left her with eight orphans.

"What am I going to do?" she pleaded. Her son was on his death bed. "A terrible cough," she explained. "It's whattayacallit tuberculosis." All of her kids had died, she said. Not natural. Better she should have died than her daughter-in-law, she whined.

Noon comes and goes. What's time mean when there's no phone to ring, no fax to send? Even cellulars don't function out here. Time in Reality is carried by wind and depends on the speed of the wind on any given day.

Today, the air hangs in place, waiting alongside me in a war of attrition. When hunger pangs develop, I suck on a grapefruit and feel that recurring sensation of worry vibrations tugging at my liver. Could the Zapatista poker game last for more than two days?

At 3:30 in the afternoon I feel like crying, so I smile and force myself into conversation with an eleven-year-old kid who wants to know how much a VW Combi costs and what renting a car means.

Then a young man, wearing blue overalls, strides purposefully toward us. He asks me if I am the *periodista*. I nod. He tells us where to be—a ten minute walk—at four o'clock. We spring into action—camera, tapes, still camera, film, notebook, notes for questions—adrenalin flowing.

At 4:05 two men wearing ski masks and carrying semi-automatic weapons walk into sight. One of them smokes a pipe. "*Buenas tardes,*" he says, shaking my hand, smiling through his mud-colored ski mask. He puts his pipe in one hand and cradles his gun in the other. His bodyguard brings two benches for us to sit on and we begin our conversation, which would last until it got dark and then continue the next day.

I finally have my meeting with Subcomandante Insurgente Marcos, Zapatista leader, poet, communicator extraordinaire, from the jungles of Chiapas. We have only an hour of daylight, so we get right into the interview.

I ask Marcos about his thinking at the time of the rebellion, January 1, 1994. He responds in Spanish. "We think that when the uprising took place on the first of January, the globalization process, which coincided with Mexico's formal incorporation into

NAFTA, meant the sacrifice of a part of humanity. In our case, it meant the sacrifice of the indigenous, of all the indigenous Mexicans but particularly the indigenous Chiapans," he tells me. "What neo-liberalism has done—the process of world globalization in NAFTA—is to eliminate a part of this population, annihilating them, wiping them from the face of the Earth.

"So, this is what we're looking at when we say, 'Enough already.' Our revolution is a revolution of words, to say, 'Here we are.' Our unique way to make this country and this world remember us, paradoxically, is by hiding ourselves. In order to show who we are, we hide, by wearing ski masks, inside a clandestine organization, using this ambiguous method to tell the country, 'We are many, we are millions, and this country is forgetting about us.'

"This cry begets not so much sympathy, as empathy. We get on the same wavelength as peasant movements and ethnic minorities from other parts of the world. In this sense, without explicitly proposing it, the Zapatista Army's message is converted into a world message, in that the oblivion suffered by the indigenous Chiapans is the same suffered by indigenous or ethnic groups in other parts of the world.

"In one way or another, it's a warning to this globalization process and to the entire world: You cannot forget a part of yourself in each project you make. The project of the future, no matter how modern, has to incorporate its past, has to incorporate its history, and he who forgets his history has to pay for it—like the neo-liberal regimes in Mexico are paying now."

I ask *"el sup"* about the social conditions of the Chiapans prior to the rebellion.

"The Indian wasn't just the citizen relegated to the lowest level. Rather, the indigenous Mexican was sub-human, not even enjoying the possibility of the cellar. In the case of the indigenous, they didn't even have the possibility of beginning to climb the educational staircase, which is the social ladder. They can't even climb the ladder of life. There isn't a family that hasn't lost a quarter or more of its children; dead in the period from birth to age five.

"This is the social-ideological basis that made it possible, on the first of January, 1994, for an army of a thousand indigenous people, poorly armed, badly trained, ill-disciplined, malnourished, poorly-equipped, to challenge a powerful army—a government at the height of its world renown, the government of Salinas de Gortari—and to challenge the entire world in the same way.

"Only a life-or-death perspective could take the indigenous groups to such a radical step— armed insurrection. Maybe if the indigenous people only lacked expectations for educational achievement, or recognized that their social conditions wouldn't allow them to improve their lives, they would have opted for other means, but they didn't have another possibility. Before the uprising, they only had the possibility of not living—of dying and dying needlessly.

"The racism used against the indigenous Chiapans is very similar to apartheid in South Africa. It's just less acknowledged here. Until 1993 a chicken, a hen, was worth more than the life of an indigenous person. Until not long ago, the indigenous in San Cristobal de las Casas couldn't walk on the sidewalk; they had to walk in the street, and they were scorned. They were despised simply because they looked Indian. Anybody not able to speak proper Spanish— meaning able to get proper schooling, besides being dark-skinned, short-statured, and dressed in a particular way— couldn't go into certain places.

"They were treated like animals. And according to what the landowners say, not even like an animal because an animal is worth more. In this sense, the death of an indigenous person didn't even count. If your mule died, you acknowledged it. You had a mule and now you don't. The indigenous people died and no one noticed.

"This is the history of the indigenous in Mexico. They've never been taken into account. On the scale of values in modern Mexico, indigenous people rate zero, lower even than an animal."

At this point, a military spotter plane dives toward us, possibly drawn by the sun reflector we're using.

"Smile," Marcos says, and reminds us that the plane has a camera. Marcos, his bodyguard, and our camera crew move under the eaves of a nearby building. When the plane flies out of sight, we resume.

I ask whether the indigenous can maintain their identity without land.

"No, the concept of land for indigenous people goes beyond what the land produces; or even land as a giver of life itself. It's not the same relationship as it is with a peasant, although his relationship with the land is very similar, in that it gives him a livelihood, roots, a goal in life. For the Indian, land also links him with history. I'm not referring to only the land he works but also the land where he lives, his community and his mountains, his rivers. It is the reference to his historic past that is not limited to something that has already passed, but it is something that is still happening."

Then I ask him about his view of President Clinton and U.S. policy toward Mexico. He answers now in broken and accented English.

"When Clinton supports the Mexican government, Zedillo's government, the U.S. government is supporting its own future problems, because the lack of democracy in Mexico means lack of justice and liberty. This increases the Mexican people's sense of instability, anxiety, and then they must go to another land to find the things they cannot find in their own land.

"I mean, when Mr. Clinton supports the facade of democracy in Mexico, he is supporting the growth of immigration to the United States from Mexico. A lot of people will go across the border because there is no democracy here, no liberty, no justice. The Mexican government doesn't do anything to resolve these problems, only increases repression with the military and police force. The military and police are corrupted by the drug traffic, and the U.S. government knows it.

"What we want in Mexico is democracy, liberty, and justice. The United States can deal with Mexico about immigration, drugs, and crime better by supporting the efforts of the Mexican people for democracy. A better border wall between Mexico and the U.S. is one constructed by democracy, liberty, and justice. We are not looking to threaten or embarrass the United States. We are looking to save our country and tell our story.

"The problem is that the U.S. government has forgotten the story of Mexico, and this is a mistake that all the American people will pay for. When the government of the United State makes a foreign policy mistake, the government doesn't pay the debt; the debt is paid by the American people.

"Each year immigration grows, and each year U.S. taxpayers pay more to solve this problem. But this problem doesn't get solved, because the problem is not in the United States, or on the U.S.-Mexican border. The problem is in Mexico. And the American people's effort to try to solve this should be directed to help the Mexican people, not help the Mexican government.

"When the American government gives money to the Mexican government, that money doesn't go to the Mexican people; it stays in the Mexican government. So poverty remains, and grows and grows and grows."

I wonder whether the Zapatistas represent a threat to the United States.

"Even in spite of our guns, we are not a threat to the United States, not even a threat to the Mexican government. Our guns are only a way of saying, 'Hey, here we are! Remember us? Don't forget us.'

"We are not terrorists. We don't have nuclear bombs. We only have the truth of our words, and we are making one prophecy to you, the American people: Your future problems are in Mexico, and to solve these problems you must help the Mexican people. I repeat, not the Mexican government but the Mexican people."

Another plane dives down. The sun has dipped behind the Blue Mountain, the wildest part of the jungle, "*el sup*" informs us. We turn the camera off. "We'll finish tomorrow," he says, shaking hands, "between 9 and 10." He and his bodyguard turn and begin their trek from Reality, the village, to their camp. We return to our vehicle, store the camera and tapes and make our way to Jorge's hut for our second meal of the day.

I cannot see by the light of the candles inside the kitchen what else but beans is floating in the bowl. A burned scrambled egg soaked in lemon juice, salt and a hot pepper, wrapped in a flaky tortilla placate my hunger. I dip the dry corn meal cake into the bean juice, hoping not to pick up any cling-ons. I drink the lukewarm, overly sweet coffee, tell the Señora how wonderful everything is and listen to the others converse about Reality.

Just as Marcos said, each family seems to have lost its share of kids, mostly between birth and five years old: fever, cough, diarrhea. With limited vocabulary and poor syntax in Spanish, the villagers nevertheless talk politics. They understand that former President Salinas' revision of Article 27 of the Constitution removed protection from their land—their life, their identity, their future. Under the revised law, there will be no land for their children and their grandchildren.

It is hardly a secret that this village is Zapatista territory. The army sends regular motorized convoys through La Realidad several times a week. Low-flying military planes and helicopters remind the villagers: "We're watching you."

Another cool night, but not cool enough to inhibit the ticks that crawl under my socks and sweat pants to gnaw at my flesh. At four thirty A.M., a horn blows, and I incorporate Yom Kippur into my dream, but when I sit up I hear the sound again. The women have already begun to do their chores. And at six more than a hundred men appear, with machetes, and begin a collective lawn mowing on all the village greenery. They finish within an hour.

Soon after, the ram's horn, called *el cacho*, sounds again and I ask the hornblower if he could repeat the blow so we could film him. He says we must ask permission. Ask Maxi. No, says the head man, the horn blowing calls the assembly; it's not for filming.

By noon, Marcos' advance man shows up and we complete the interview.

I ask him about his reputation as a "post-modern" revolutionary, one who uses drama and a sense of humor— something notably absent in other revolutionary movements.

"Believe me, the only way to survive here in the Lacondon jungle is to laugh. You have to have a well-developed sense of humor or be completely nuts. Or maybe in our case, both of these things. What we tried to do was to be spontaneous, that is to say, don't reflect too much, don't predict things, and I think that is what has given coherence to what we can do."

I ask him whether it's difficult to have a personal life as a guerrilla, or whether he's turned into a different person.

"I've turned into three people. There are three Marcoses: the Marcos of the past who has a past, the Marcos of the mountains before the first of January, and post January 1 Marcos. Of those, the most important one is the Marcos who is the product of all the others up until now. It is the Marcos of after the first of January.

"That's why people say it doesn't matter who Marcos is: Marcos is a symbol, he means something we have constructed. And that's the truth. In reality, the Marcos everyone knows, the Marcos of the ski mask, is someone in turn constructed by this ski mask, and who reflects a mountain of aspirations, and who has nothing to do with the person that is behind the ski mask.

"But someone is behind the ski mask," he laughs, "and that's the truth, and that Marcos is the one who spent twelve years in the mountains before the first of January, who was born out of the corpse of the civilian Marcos."

I mention that Fidel Castro once said there is no life that requires greater sacrifice than guerilla life.

"It was a very tough time, really very difficult. I don't know how to measure deprivation because seeing the indigenous conditions I would say that if anyone lives worse than guerillas it is the indigenous people here.

"But it was a very difficult situation especially for someone from the city. The only thing that allowed you to survive was the hope that something would come from everything we were doing. It was an irrational expectation, totally loony, because there was nothing, absolutely nothing, that would validate what you were doing— not world news, nor anything.

"We are talking about a group of four, five, six people in the mid-1980s, and we kept repeating to ourselves all day, all night, 'We are good. This was what we had to do.' But there was nothing outside of that to confirm that what you were doing made sense.

"Moreover, the mountain was rejecting you. The mountain made you hungry, sick. It pushed rain and cold on you. The aggression of animals, insects, all this was saying, 'Go, go, you have no business here.'

"And the entire world was telling you the same thing. The socialist camp was collapsing, the armed struggle route was completely abandoned, and you were like some nuts clinging to a dream, dreaming because that was the truth.

"You were dreaming that what you were doing was going to be good for something, and we didn't have ambitious dreams. Don't think that we were fantasizing about seizing power and then becoming great presidents or emulating Castro or Lenin or whatever. We were thinking that at least we were going to help the indigenous people transform their lives in a radical and irreversible way so that the past would not return."

He poses for photos with my wife and me. I ask him what size boots he wears, noticing that his are shredded. He says, "Forget it. I have a sentimental attachment to these."

We depart from Reality in late afternoon. I feel mixed emotions. The forty-three red welts and bumps, some with stingers left in them, will remain for only about three weeks, but the other memories will stick.

The road has suffered more rain, thus there is more dangerous, slippery mud. Carlos navigates the Combi, whose steering grows increasingly unresponsive, through perilous pits and caverns. Then, just after we drive through the ghost village of Guadalupe Tepeyac, we meet a road-fixing project—dump trucks loaded with dirt and a giant bulldozer. The army after all, like the Pony Express, has to get through.

A dump truck in front of us tries to turn around and backs its rear wheels into a ditch. It now blocks the entire narrow road. The driver then tries to jump it out by putting the vehicle in low and revving the accelerator. Because of all the weight in the back, he breaks the axle. Behind us is a truckload of village men, presumably Zapatistas, then another dump truck, then an army vehicle with a platoon of soldiers.

I contemplate a variety of scenarios that range from armed confrontation between the soldiers and Zapatistas behind us to slow death by starvation. The soldiers and Zapatistas avert their eyes when the patrol walks by. I note how much alike their young indigenous faces are. Then the bulldozer operator goes into motion, miraculously turns the dump truck and points it downhill, and pushes it onto the shoulder just enough for us to pass. "*Buey*," (Ox) screams Carlos the cameraman as we pass the driver who has broken the truck's axle.

On the road we film an Indian girl, who appears to be no more than 12, carrying a load of wood that a lumber jack would find difficult to hoist. Her stoic young face is a thousand years old. She has been carrying the wood for centuries.

Three hours and much kidney exercise later we arrive at the paved road. We find the phone and call home to ascertain that our kids are alive and well, concerns shared by the people with whom we have spent a few days, who don't have phones, but may have kids living in Los Angeles or Houston, people who cling to a culture that determines life according to Nature's dictates, an organic life style, tough, cruel and Spartan. They and their ancestors have fed themselves and others for over a millennium. Now they face extinction, by what the "*el sup*" calls neo-liberalism.

"Hey," he reminded, "don't forget about us!"

Saul Landau

Agreement in Chiapas

February 15, 1996

Yesterday, in a small town named San Andres Larrainzar, about 30 miles form the old colonial capital of San Cristobal de las Casas, a ski-masked Zapatista commander named Tacho announced that 96% of the Mayan Indian population of southeastern Chiapas had endorsed an agreement with the Mexican government.

This is a victory for Mexico's indigenous people. Two years and forty-five days after the Zapatistas seized eight cities in Chiapas, the government has bowed to one key demand: autonomy.

The government agreed that Indians have a right to govern themselves under their customs and traditions, that their languages have equal weight in formal education and that they will have representatives in local, state and national legislatures.

The agreement also calls for renovation of the court system and prosecutor's office, the agencies used for decades by ranchers and political bosses to put Indian troublemakers in jail on phony charges. The agreement calls for the establishment of a real human rights office, not another government front organization. And, the pact allows Zapatistas to run for election without belonging to an established political party—a break from past rules. This means that the Zapatista Army of National Liberation can convert itself into a political force, one that represents Indians, and also play a lead role as an agency for national reform: an immense political victory for the Zapatistas.

For President Zedillo, the accord offers a chance to apply make-up to Mexico's battered face, a positive event to counteract revelations of murder, drug dealing and theft of public funds.

The agreement doesn't change everyday Indian village life because the government has not conceded on Zapatista claims to possess communal land in perpetuity and have access to additional lands for future generations. The agreement does, however, call for the creation of a land disputes settlement office to hear cases involving conflicting claims.

The accord creates an atmosphere of peace in an area that has seen perpetual conflict. But don't hold your breath waiting for the Mexican government to cede real autonomy to Indian people. It will require continual struggle for the Mayans to regain control over the resources on their land; like natural gas, oil and precious wood and metals.

As long as President Zedillo refuses to discuss his central economic strategy of making the country a part of the global economy, the native people will not have security. NAFTA has failed, but the globalization policy prevails. This means Mexico's land and resources are being converted into merchandise, available to international investors. This economic strategy is incompatible with indigenous peoples' rights. And the Zapatistas know it. So, for those resisting globalization, take a sip of celebratory champagne, but put the cork back in. There's lots to do before we reverse the globalization strategy, dismantle corporate rule and democratize the economy. In the meantime, "¡*Viva Zapata!*"

Saul Landau

Privatizing

April 10, 1996

Delegates converged on Mexico's Lacondon jungle last week to discuss neo-liberalism, the market model that has become the axiom of the new world order. The 1994 Zapatista rebellion against this international trading culture has spread in Latin America. Mass protests erupted in La Paz, Bolivia, Caracas, and Asuncion, Paraguay, in which outraged citizens demanded an end to privatization, the core of neo-liberalism.

The term refers to the behavior of supersalesmen disguised as politicians—like former Mexican President Carlos Salinas, Peruvian President Alberto Fujimori or Argentina's Carlos Menem. These new-age virtuosos sold off public property, balanced their budgets by cutting basic services to the poor and claimed they had made their nations competitive and efficient.

Wipe away this cloud of business jargon and you discover that these elected officials cum auctioneers handed over their people's patrimony. State-owned steel mills, banks, airlines and utilities became private property.

Corruption surrounding these sales has become legendary. The auctioneers over- or under-price, play insider trading games, cut deals with relatives or newly bought—I mean acquired— friends.

Where did this money come from in such poor countries, you ask? Well, don't ask. Where did the profits from these sales go? Salinas' big brother Raul had stashed tens of millions in foreign bank accounts, under aliases—but he planned to use it as venture capital, to create jobs.

It took time until people caught on. Devaluation and rising unemployment make excellent teachers. The media revealed a variety of boondoggles, the public experienced the deterioration of services and quality once the private sharks got a hold of the public meat. The privatizers extracted immense profits by firing workers, cutting down on necessary maintenance costs of once-public highways and utilities and by gutting airline routes and services.

When these newly-privatized industries ran into financial trouble, the very government that sold them off as examples of its efficiency had to bail them out. The taxpayers had to cough up more money—and received nothing in return.

Currently Bolivians, Venezuelans and Mexicans, including sectors of their armies, demand a halt to plans to sell off their nation's oil wealth. In Paraguay, workers staged strikes that forced the government to postpone privatization deals. Popular pressure in Brazil forced the government to halt the sell-off a state-owned mining company.

The supersalesmen masquerading as presidents proudly wear their democracy labels on their tailored suits. Washington loves them, despite the immeasurable harm they have done to their people. We read in the prestige media that free market economics is the best and only model available. Twenty-five years ago Brazilian President Medici commented on the immense suffering that came from his applying the neo-liberal model. "What I have done," he declared, "is very good for Brazil, but not so good for Brazilians." Amen!

Saul Landau

Mexican Political Prisoners

May 14, 1996

Last week Mexican Judge Juan Manuel Alcantara sentenced Javier Elorriaga to 13 years on charges of terrorism, conspiracy and rebellion against the government. Sebastian Entzin, an 18-year-old Tzeltal Indian, received six years for conspiracy. Both were accused of being Zapatistas.

I talked to Elorriaga via cellular phone. From his jail cell in Chaipas, he said that the U.S. public should know that in February 1995 army officials detained him as he emerged from the Lacondon jungle where, as part of a TV crew, he had been filming with Subcomandante Marcos, the leader of Zapatista Army of National Liberation. The army had neither the authority to arrest him nor a proper detention order, he said.

The government's key witness, Salvador Morales Garibay, never appeared at Elorriaga's trial. The defense lawyers never had the chance to cross examine him. The judge admitted into evidence against Elorriaga the confession of his wife, Gloria Benavides. She was arrested also and claimed that the police had tortured her to get the confession. The judge, in her case, refused to admit the confession as evidence.

Flawed procedures in this case go hand in hand with substantive irregularities. The Mexican government holds talks with Zapatista leaders, grants them amnesty and yet charges two other people with less rank and power than the ones at the negotiating table with being Zapatista leaders.

Marcos pulled out of the talks after the sentencing of Elorriaga and Entzin. Sixty thousand troops patrol the Chiapas jungle area where the Zapatista loyalists live. Cattle barons, sugar cane ranchers and coffee estate owners demand the government wipe out the Zapatista military organization and remove their supporters.

A New York bank adviser offered similar advice. Mexican military officials and hard-line ruling party pols, frustrated over the lack of resolution, want President Zedillo to use force. As the

Mexican economy drags and street crime grows, mini political revolts and rebellions erupt throughout the country. In Tepotzlan, against a golf course; in Tabasco, against oil drilling; in Morelos, against unjust police actions; everywhere against unemployment. On May Day, hundreds of thousands of Mexico City unionists defied orders from Fidel Velasquez, the 95-year-old George Meany of Mexican labor, and marched to protest government policies.

Contrary to neo-liberal prophecies, investment does not pour into unstable and lawless Mexico, even though President Zedillo made all the right "free market, punish the poor" moves. As the model fails, the military option looms large. The tough guys say that by making war on the Zapatistas at least the unloved Zedillo would be feared.

Readers can write Zedillo. Demand that he release Elorriaga and Entzin. Send copies to John Shattuck, Assistant Secretary of State for Human Rights. Write your Senators and Representatives to pressure Zedillo to free the political prisoners and resume meaningful negotiations—not war with the Zapatistas.

Saul Landau

Mexico Teachers Strike

June 1, 1996

During the last week of May, hundreds of Mexico City schools closed because some one third of the teachers went on strike. Dissident sections of the National Teaching Workers Union have already forced school closings in Guerrero, Michoacan and Tamaulipas.

The teachers demanded higher wages to meet rising living costs, and they were declaring their independence from the official teachers union. Like millions of Mexicans, these teachers have had it with the new economic model that charts its destructive course inside the corridors of the old and super corrupt political system.

Why the strikes of teachers, bus drivers, oil workers; protests by small business people; uprisings and land takeovers by peasants and indigenous people? Twenty years ago, Mexico had a functioning fascist model. The State and the ruling PRI party spread some wealth throughout various sectors of the population. The president acted as a dictator—for six years. He and his cohorts dominated the nation's economic development and limited the tears in the social fabric. To work, to farm, to succeed in business one belonged to the official organization—of teachers, peasants, bricklayers; or to the appropriate business association. Dissenters suffered prison—or worse. The system excluded millions of people, but compared to other Latin American models, the old Mexican model offered considerable stability.

In those days, unemployed or landless Mexicans used the U.S. border as a relatively painless escape valve.

By migrating, some unemployed or recently landless Mexicans supported their families. The money they sent home enriched Mexico's foreign currency supply.

Then in 1982, besieged by a newly acquired debt and unable to meet the payments, Mexico's leaders adopted free market economics—but without making corresponding political changes.

The state began to sell off its enterprises to a few lucky recipients while it reduced subsidies to the poor and middle classes. But it maintained its official unions and the organizations that held the power of access for Mexican workers, peasants, businessmen and teachers. The State and party no longer deliver the goods, but still demand allegiance from the populace they have abandoned.

On May 1, despite orders from labor tsar Fidel Velasquez, hundreds of thousands of unionists marched in protest against the government and its official union. Last week, riot police charged the striking teachers in Mexico City. Blood flowed after the police finished wielding their batons.

The teachers' dispute is part of a larger conflict over the nature of Mexico's social contract. President Zedillo has thus far refused to yield to protests or uprisings. Prices rise. Wages fall and the peso buckles under the weight of the seemingly endless crisis.

Under the neo-liberal model, the president must turn his back on teachers, who claim they can't live on their old salaries. Some of the most militant will join a growing number of dissidents in prison.

"The Mexican Miracle"—on Paper

January 21, 1997

Treasury Secretary Robert Rubin and our new president, Bill Clinton, have hailed Mexico's early multi-billion dollar repayment of our 1995 bailout loan. This proves, said the taciturn Clinton, that our policy worked. Mexico has recovered, announced Rubin. We even made a profit on the loan, crowed Clinton.

Our leaders described a Mexico that opened two factories a day, that employed ever more workers, that had won itself fabulous credit ratings in Europe—where the Mexican government went to borrow the money to repay the loan, so it could then borrow even more money.

Everything Clinton and Rubin said was true—well, sort of. Two new factories do open daily—but they're foreign owned and near the U.S. border. They work on the dollar, not peso economy. Neither man mentioned that two Mexican-owned factories close every day. According to the January 14 *Financial Times*, for every worker hired by a foreign maquila, one worker employed by a Mexican patron is laid off. The 3233 maquiladoras bring a work force of mostly rural people, whose infertile land no longer feeds them.

Clinton and Rubin's portrait is Mexico as viewed from Wall Street, where investors look at figures that have little relationship to what any sensible person sees and hears in that country.

Two Mexicos, the one with the successful dollarized economy and the other with the failed peso.

Investors pour dollars into the border factories, which buy heavy equipment from the United States to make the chips, semi conductors, car batteries, textiles etc. Then, the profits move right across the border with the goods. It's free trade. Dollars in, dollars out.

One Mexico is dying, another is being born—fathered by foreign investors. Yes, millions have found factory jobs that pay wages higher than in other parts of their country, but the border towns also have a higher cost of living than the rest of Mexico.

Mexico's national debt is crippling. Away from the buzzing border, unemployment and underemployment statistics remain frighteningly high. Social unrest breaks out daily in different forms. Street sweepers from Tabasco stage hunger strikes, garbage collectors call a wildcat action, leaving the capital city with an even greater stench than usual.

Peasant uprisings, teachers' marches, environmental protests—more than 3000 alone in Mexico City last year. Corruption remains rampant, crime has reached all time high levels. Prosecutors and investigative reporters delving into drug trafficking or political assassinations get bumped off routinely .

Environmental dangers have also reached peaks. Air quality in Mexico City is beyond impossible, soil erosion threatens the very future of agriculture in the nation.

So the question becomes: who are you going to believe—Clinton and Rubin, who read the figures about loan repayments and the foreign-owned factory boom or your own eyes and ears?

Saul Landau

Weekend in Juarez

April 28, 1998

I enter Ciudad Juarez from El Paso, Texas, an American city with a population of 600,000, about 70 percent of it Mexican or, excuse me Mexican American. Juarez, population 2 million, has the proverbial strip with bars, sex clubs, hookers outside.

Juarez has a booming economy—thanks to the maquilas, the foreign-owned factories that make parts for U.S.-based plants—like Ford, GM, RCA, and big textile and computer companies that make items that we touch, wear or use to compose radio commentaries and even broadcast them. One RCA worker took me to the top of a barren hill where the poor reside.

The rich live on the flats—where there is access to water and the streets are paved. After fighting over unpaved streets filled with protruding rocks, we reach his hand-built, wood-stripped shack, covered with sheets of cardboard. His pregnant wife and small child stare at a TV soap opera in the dirt-floored bedroom. They share with his brother, sister-in-law and their two children a tiny kitchen with a used fridge and stove and a jerry built ceiling light. No living room, dining room or bathroom. All seven share a tiny outhouse, with a crude door built from scrap metal. Like the neighbors, he borrows electric power from a nearby line. One guy recently touched the wrong wire and got fried. Electricity is expensive, except for the maquilas. His wife carries water from a nearby pipe and stores it in barrels.

Outside the wind blows dust. The cardboard covers holes in the wooden walls. I meet Evangelina, mother of a disappeared woman. She cries as she gives me the details. One day she didn't return. Over the last three years more than 100 young women have been abducted. Most have been raped, tortured and then mutilated. The police arrested some poor joker and announced that they'd caught the killer. A fresh female corpse then turns up—killed in the same way.

"What connection has this got with the maquilas?" I ask Judith, who runs the Human Rights center.

"The maquila culture kills the family," she says. "Now, we have youth gangs dealing drugs for the cartels, robbing, or smuggling. Killing each other. Free trade means pushing small farmers off their land or forcing the closure of Mexican-owned factories. We have 2 million in Juarez, but no facilities to house or school them or treat their diseases.

"Yes," she says, "free trade is great—if you're an American plant manager and commute from El Paso."

She shows me photos of young women who have turned up dead or are still missing. Evangelina points to the photo of her daughter. Tears flow. She leaves to care for her mother-less grandchildren. I take a deep breath and suck polluted air into my lungs.

Yeah, it's the new order. God help us!

Saul Landau

Bishop Ruiz Resigns

June 12, 1998

Blood flows in Chiapas. U.S. newspapers report soldiers and police fighting leftist rebels. They don't report, however, that the Mexican government destroyed negotiating efforts and forced the resignation of the one man trusted by the native people. He could no longer in good faith act as mediator to a dishonest government.

In late September 1993, I met a man wearing an old, shiny blue suit in Washington, DC. Bishop Samuel Ruiz, from San Cristobal de las Casas, Chiapas, Mexico, had come to Washington to receive the Letelier Moffitt human rights award, given in honor of our slain colleagues Orlando Letelier and Ronni Moffitt. Both died in 1976 when Chilean General Pinochet's agents detonated a bomb under their car.

Bishop Ruiz said, "If the Bible says that the meek shall inherit the earth, obviously you cannot take away their land." That sentence summed up the issue between the indigenous Mayan people and the rapacious Chiapas land barons—supported by the government and the PRI, Mexico's long-standing official political party.

Three months later, on January 1, 1994, reactionaries accused Samuel Ruiz of having instigated the uprising of thousands of Mayans who seized eight Chiapas cities and issued a challenge to the neo-liberal ideologues. Indigenous people will resist the globalizers.

Bishop Ruiz received death threats. Ironically, the Bishop differed with the Zapatistas precisely over the issue of violence. Subcomandante Marcos, Zapatista leader, said that the Bishop stood for non-violent mobilization. "But non-violence had led to prison or the grave," said Marcos. "We chose something more radical."

When I filmed in Chiapas, I suspected that beneath the trademark ski masks were several ex-catechists whom Bishop Ruiz and his staff had trained for three decades to organize

231

indigenous people to resist those who planned to evict them from their land.

Ruiz discovered in Catholic law a precedent for communal land holding. His team found records of Mayan titles that existed prior to the Spanish conquest.

When the Zapatista–government impasse arose after twelve days of fighting in 1994, Bishop Ruiz agreed to mediate. The Indians called him *Tatic*, "Revered Father." But President Zedillo reneged on the settlement his own team had signed. Instead, he sent the army to wage a war of attrition to destroy the Zapatistas and erase resistance. By practicing bad faith, the Mexican government pushed Bishop Ruiz to resign. They had made a mockery out of negotiations.

So, headlines unfold. More Indians die. The Mexican government employs tens of thousands of troops with tanks and aircraft to maintain its illegitimate hold over the Mayan area of Chiapas. It also complains that it doesn't have the resources to employ firefighters to extinguish the deadly blaze burning in central Mexico. Priorities?

How ironic. The mediocre President of Mexico meets with the mediocre President of the United States. Yet, Bishop Ruiz had to resign. I picture him travelling through Mayan villages counseling people to keep the faith, in God, yes, but also in their own ability to act as subjects of their own history.

Saul Landau

Reasons for Optimism
on Mexico's Economy?

June 23, 1998

Welcome to my business report on the rock-solid, democracy-bound, no-holds-barred free market economy of Mexico, our beloved trading partner.

Over the past month, Mexico's stock market has taken a bit of a plunge, well, just a 20 percent drop. You know stock markets—unpredictable and fickle.

In mid June, the peso deteriorated, from 8.3 to over 9 per dollar. Peso weakening shows no sign of reversing itself. But nostalgia has no place in business. Ah, the good old days of 1994 when 3.3 pesos equaled a dollar. Hey, think of the maquiladora owners! They pay labor in pesos, which means they get more work out of workers for less money—especially since wages have not risen to coincide with the recent peso dive.

Mexico has also taken a recent hit in income of several billion dollars when oil prices dropped.

In addition, the media has exposed Mexico's banking system, not just for laundering drug money—someone has to do that—but for loans among bankers and irregularities in giving credits to those companies connected with the banks. The liabilities or bad debts of Mexico's big banks run over $65 billion, according to *Proceso* magazine.

President Zedillo has proposed a bill to pass this debt on to the public—to stabilize the banking system of course. But Mexico's Congress—even members of Zedillo's own PRI party—has shown reluctance to pass Zedillo's plan. Public opinion polls indicate that the public doesn't want to bail out the bankers. Indeed, they would rather send them to prison—as details surface of some entrepreneurs'—how shall I say it—less-than-savory transactions. Ah, the price of democracy!

Under these circumstances, Zedillo faces an uphill climb. His firefighters have yet to extinguish the blaze burning in Mexico's forests. In Chiapas, Zedillo spends a fortune maintaining an army of 70,000 soldiers, but with little hope for peace in the near future. In June, the army participated in another mini massacre, in Guerrero, executing eight people—supposedly in the course of repressing an armed guerrilla force.

Problems? Imagine a crime wave that has affected one in four Mexico City residents and now has spread throughout Mexico. The police cannot solve the problem because often they are directly linked to the criminals. Poverty—some 60 million very poor people—and the displacement of millions from rural areas have created a horrendous social mess for a government suffering from overwhelming debt, a banking crisis and several armed uprisings.

But investors should feel optimistic. After all, President Clinton has assured us that Mexico's economic future is bright and the NAFTA (free trade) agreement with Mexico and Canada as responsible for Mexico's buoyant economy. I must have missed some positive indicators, since we all know that Bill Clinton never steers us wrong.

Index

About the Author

As an author, filmmaker and political activist, Saul Landau has won an Emmy, a George Polk Award, the First Amendment Award and the Letelier-Moffitt award for human rights. He has also won many prizes at film festivals for his more than forty films, which include *Fidel*, *The Uncompromising Revolution*, *Paul Jacobs and the Nuclear Gang* (with Jack Willis), *Brazil: Report on Torture* (with Haskell Wexler) and *The Sixth Sun*. Most of these films are available on video through the Cinema Guild in New York City. Among Landau's ten books are *Assassination on Embassy Row* (with John Dinges), *The Dangerous Doctrine: National Security and U.S. Foreign Policy*, *The Guerilla Wars of Central America*, *Hot Air: A Radio Diary* and *My Dad Was Not Hamlet* (poems). Landau has been a fellow of the Institute for Policy Studies in Washington, D.C. for twenty-six years and of the Amsterdam Transnational Institute since 1974. He is currently the Hugh O. La Bounty Chair of Interdisciplinary Applied Knowledge at California State Polytechnic University, Pomona. He continues to air his commentaries on Pacifica Radio Network News.

For More Great Books and Information

Award-Winning Common Courage Press has been publishing exposés from authors on the front lines since 1991. Authors include

- Louise Armstrong
- Judi Bari
- Peter Breggin
- Joanna Cagan
- Noam Chomsky
- Neil deMause
- Laura Flanders
- Jennifer Harbury

- Jeffrey Moussaieff Masson
- Margaret Randall
- John Ross
- Ken Silverstein
- Norman Solomon
- Cornel West
- Howard Zinn
- and many others

Also available: the dynamite **The Real Stories Series** of small books from **Odonian Press**—including titles from Noam Chomsky and Gore Vidal.

FOR BULK DISCOUNTS CALL 800-497-3207

For catalogs and updates, call **800-497-3207** or email **orders-info@commoncouragepress.com**.

Send us your email address to get updates by email!

For more information, visit our web site at **www.commoncouragepress.com**.

Write us at
Common Courage Press
Box 702
Monroe, ME 04951